MW01068410

# INVESTING
# REDEFINED

# INVESTING REDEFINED

A Proven Investment Approach
*for a* Changing World

## RANDY SWAN

RIVER GROVE
BOOKS

This publication is designed to provide accurate and authoritative information in regard to the subject matter covered. It is sold with the understanding that the publisher and author are not engaged in rendering legal, accounting, or other professional services. If legal advice or other expert assistance is required, the services of a competent professional should be sought.

Published by River Grove Books
Austin, TX
www.rivergrovebooks.com

Copyright ©2019 Swan Global Investments

"Investing Redefined" is a wholly-owned trademark of Swan Global Investments, LLC.

All rights reserved.

Thank you for purchasing an authorized edition of this book and for complying with copyright law. No part of this book may be reproduced, stored in a retrieval system, or transmitted by any means, electronic, mechanical, photocopying, recording, or otherwise, without written permission from the copyright holder.

Distributed by River Grove Books

For permission to include copyrighted material, grateful acknowledgment is made to the following sources:
Chapter 1
"Maximum Drawdowns for Major Asset Classes Over the Last Decade," from "Must-know: Minimizing ETF losses by observing max drawdowns." 19 December, 2013. https://marketrealist.com/2013/12/first-bridge-etf-landscape-risk-report-loss-minimization. Reproduced by permission of Aniket Ullal.
Chapter 2
"Entitlement Spending As Pct Government: US from FY 1900 to FY 2020," from US Government Spending. Accessed 25 October, 2018. https://www.usgovernmentspending.com/spending_chart_1900_2020USp_XXs2li011tcn_00t10t40t_Entitlement_Spending_as_Pct_GDP. Reproduced by the permission of the compiler, Christopher Chantrill.
"Estimates of the U.S. Population, by Age, 1950 to 2050," from Pew Research Center. 30 January, 2014. http://www.pewglobal.org/2014/01/30/global-population/. Reproduced by permission of Pew Research Center.
"Real Federal Debt with Estimates through 2018" from "Debt, Taxes and Politics: An Updated Perspective on Federal Tax History." 13 November, 2017. https://www.advisorperspectives.com/dshort/updates/2017/11/13/debt-taxes-and-politics-an-updated-perspective-on-federal-tax-history. Reproduced by permission of Advisor Perspectives.
Chapter 3
"Stock Market Valuation Based on S&P Companies' Book Values and Dividends," Elliott Wave Theorist. June 2018. Reproduced by permission of Elliott Wave International.
Chapter 4
"Risks to the Global Outlook," from "World Economic Outlook, April 2016: Too Slow for Too Long." 12 April, 2016. https://www.imf.org/en/Publications/WEO/Issues/2016/12/31/World-Economic-Outlook-April-2016-Too-Slow-for-Too-Long-43653. Reproduced by permission of the International Monetary Fund.
"How Much Money Americans Have in Savings, 2014–2018," from GOBankingRates.com. 21 December 2018. Reproduced by permission of GOBankingRates.com. https://www.gobankingrates.com/saving-money/savings-advice/average-american-savings-account-balance/

Cover Design and composition by Greenleaf Book Group and Brian Phillips
Cover images © decade3d and Nokwan00, 2019. Used under license from Shutterstock.com

Publisher's Cataloging-in-Publication data is available.

Print ISBN: 978-1-63299-208-6

eBook ISBN: 978-1-63299-209-3

First Edition

# CONTENTS

# PREFACE

Driving home from work on a dreary September evening, Mary slumps behind the wheel. Through the windshield, a line of brake lights stretches as far as the eye can see. Another long Monday behind her, but plenty of traffic ahead. "At least I have only two more years until retirement," she sighs, daydreaming about how she'll spend those free hours. Then the radio announcer catches her attention. It's the bottom of the hour; time for the 5:30 p.m. news update. Mary hears the news correspondent mention something about Congress rejecting a TARP bailout. She isn't sure what that means, but the next words to come through her car's speakers are crystal clear:

> It's the biggest single-day loss for the major stock indices as investors grow increasingly concerned about a potential mortgage crisis. The Dow Jones Industrial Average fell over 778 points, or nearly 7%. The S&P 500 also recorded its largest single-day tumble, losing 8.8% of its value, down over 106 points, and the NASDAQ lost over 9%, the largest decline since 2000 . . . [1]

Mary may not understand the subtleties, but she knows the news is bad. When she gets home, she and her husband will have to talk about that retirement account.

Mary, and many investors just like her in 2008, didn't know that this was just the beginning. Chances are you were one of them, another Mary whose financial future got caught up in an inevitable and yet unpredictable market meltdown. Were you among the millions of Americans listening to the news, hoping it hadn't happened, and wondering what you could have done to protect your money?

Perhaps you remember exactly how it felt in October 2008, when the market began to sell off rapidly, finally bottoming out in March 2009—a total loss, from peak to trough, of over 50 percent for the S&P 500 Index. Major banks and investment firms went out of business; the financial world seemed to be facing Armageddon. Even after some jiggering of the markets and record intervention by Congress, the Federal Reserve, and other world central banks, the economy still fell into a recession, taking more businesses and financial dreams with it. Talk to almost anyone over the age of thirty-five, and they can describe emotional and financial scars from the 2008 Financial Crisis. Investment professionals can also recount their horror stories of dreams lost or postponed, and the arduous years of rebuilding that followed.

A decade later, these equity market indices have recovered and are pushing all-time highs. People have begun to forget the pain. They chase returns and take on risk, confident they'll be able to get out of the way of the bear next time. Wall Street calls it "dodging the falling knives." Why should anyone think they can dodge the same knives that rained down on them before? Many do, as evidenced by the industry and individuals who build portfolios the same way they did before those major market meltdowns. Doing the same thing, yet expecting a different result next time, seems like fiduciary and investor insanity.

A major flaw in industry logic argues that market risk, the inherent risk in the markets of losing the money one invests, can be dealt with through diversification across different investments and asset classes. That argument does not—has *never*—effectively limited the devastation that investors felt during crises like the dot.com bust, the recession of 2000–02, and in the 2008 Financial Crisis. The industry repeatedly labels such events "black swans" or "hundred-year storms," and then tells investors, "We'll get 'em next time." And they never quite do, do they? Investors shouldn't have to simply accept that Band-Aid of a solution.

I certainly don't. I began investing at a young age, and I learned that pain firsthand, losing over 20 percent of my money in 1987. I hate losing money, and I never accept being told to "get 'em next time." Through my career as a certified public accountant, and by witnessing how large institutions like insurance companies manage risk while always investing premiums, I began to develop a new philosophy. In 1997 I devised a better way to grow and protect my wealth. I saw that the investing landscape continually evolves in ways that necessitate a change in how investors approach the market. Put another way: The board has been changing, in permanent ways, since the late 1980s, but the industry hasn't provided new ways to play the game.

Drawing from my investing and professional background, I sought a way to define the risk of loss and directly address market risk, which the industry continually fails (or is unwilling) to do, and thereby redefine the risk/reward dynamic in investing. I call this approach the "Defined Risk Strategy," and it rests on two central pillars:

1. Remain always invested to build wealth over time.
2. Remain always hedged to define the risk and limit the effects of losing big during inevitable, yet unpredictable, times of major market stress.

I honed this strategy first with my own money, then with that of friends and family. Then I started an investment advisory firm to help investors directly. Eventually, we grew this company into an asset management firm to provide investors at large an innovative, yet commonsense, approach that investors inherently desire: a way to grow wealth without experiencing large life-altering losses—a set-it-and-forget-it type of wealth-building investment.

I offer this book to anyone who wants to better understand the combination of profound changes in the investment landscape that present daunting challenges for any investor and, therefore, sees the necessity of changing how they invest going forward to grow and protect their wealth. I will describe the rational process I used to draw the conclusions presented here and offer historical proof of efficacy for my Defined Risk Strategy (DRS). Hopefully, like me, you will discover it is a better way to invest—one that does not involve dodging bears or falling knives.

My family name, Swan, may derive from a random act of genealogy, but I see it as a fitting descriptor for my company's corporate culture and investment success. Like the elegant bird, Swan Global Investments strives to remain calm and serene on top of the water while paddling furiously underneath. A group of swans is called a "ballet," and that's how we seek to operate: all participants moving in harmony to create positive outcomes, executing the feats of precision and balance that make up any successful dance. And don't mess with a swan, either; they are known to aggressively protect their nests. At Swan Global Investments, that is where we excel. We are proud of the unique way we have developed our DRS to grow and protect our clients' nests.

The purpose of *Investing Redefined* is to invite you into our nest.

Finding the vehicle best suited to your individual investment needs and current cash flow is one of life's most daunting and important tasks. What fits a young person just out of college with a spare thousand dollars will not work for a couple approaching retirement with the last two kids in college, nor an advisor to a multibillion-dollar pension fund. Nor do these individuals favor the same investing approach. The college kid wants to download a phone app and invest the minimum's minimum. The soon-to-be retiree prefers to call his cousin's uncle's brother-in-law at the Big Investment Firm for personal advice, without clicks or buttons, for managing risk and generating retirement income. The endowment or pension fund advisor seeks out strategies that can provide consistency and repeatability through market cycles.

Most ask, "Where do I start?" Certainly, a reasonable question.

At Swan, we want you to ask, "Where do I end?"

Just like life, investing has unavoidable ups and downs. Though many fund managers try to pretend these are just "corrections," that is not how we view your nest at Swan. Since its 1792 inception, Wall Street has depended on traditional asset allocation, more recently known as Modern Portfolio Theory. Bolstered by tradition, single-focused talking points, and a system terrified of the natural and expected financial dips that can cause some level of failure, the traditional investment community has developed euphemisms (corrections, black swans, bear markets) to cover that which should be anticipated by the natural law of things. This philosophy does nothing to shield an investor's nest from those financial storms.

We don't want to fix your nest after it falls out of the tree. Instead, we want to climb the tree and tie it to the strongest branch. Think of our DRS as the rope. Many factors influence investments: politics and ideology, government intervention, environmental and international events. These macro influences affect our financial goals and aspirations but remain beyond most individuals' control. So what can you do? With the right strategy in place, you can face them head on and hedge the risks they present.

The concept of hedging has been around since western Europeans first used bushes to delineate "this is my farm and that is yours." We still use the term in a variety of ways: You can "hedge your bets," a politician can "hedge a promise," or an enemy can face a "hedge of spears." In other words, a hedge exists to mitigate risk; it creates a boundary between someone and full disaster. To hedge is to enclose yourself in a protective barrier that helps shield you from the worst possible outcome.

Our DRS uses hedging to define, or seek to limit, portfolio losses to generate consistent returns over the long term. Minimizing losses can help investors achieve long-term goals while weathering the many market cycles they will inevitably face. In protecting your capital from major losses, we believe you will be better off in the long run. Why? Investing can be a crazy ride. Sometimes investors need protection from themselves. One of the greatest threats to an investor's long-term success is a costly, emotional decision made at the wrong time. Substantial research into investor behavior demonstrates that, especially in times of market stress or uncertainty, emotions drive decisions, often to an individual's detriment. Even the best investment plan is only as good as the investor's ability to stick with it. So a strategy that hedges against big loss can help investors stay steady, avoid confusion and emotionality when the ride gets bumpy, and evade choices that result in major losses. More specifically, the DRS seeks to shield investors from the economic mulligan that occurs when markets fall and investors panic. Basically, we seek to win by not losing.

Fortunately, math supports this approach. Above all, the mathematical concept of compound interest requires time—substantial amounts of time, in fact. That means your nest egg needs to stay in the markets for quite a while to really take off and build your investments' (nest egg) value. In that substantial period of time, your investing lifetime, you will face ups and downs. Meanwhile, another mathematical principle called negative compounding dictates that the larger the loss suffered by an investment, the more time it can take to recover. If you hope to start a business, send kids to college, or buy your retirement home, a market recovery from a major loss may require more time than you have. Therefore, how you look at risk and the portfolio pie itself should be redefined.

The DRS redefines investing around what is best over the long term. It has redefined the risk/reward dynamic in equity investing. Equities (stocks) have historically been one of the best performing asset classes over time, yet they can create a bumpy ride for investors, with inevitable yet unpredictable periods of severe losses along the way.

We want investors to change the way they look at risk when constructing portfolios. The investment landscape is changing in major ways and traditional approaches have a limited ability to address those changes. We also seek to change the way investors look at returns. Long-term goals require effective long-term strategies. After all, what does a large gain in a bull market matter if you give up most of it in the next bear market? In developing the DRS, I wanted to create an approach that would give me the greatest probability to achieve my long-term goals while facing the inevitable and unpredictable market cycles—a full market cycle strategy.

A successful strategy has to live through a full market cycle (both a bull and a bear) before you consider returns. With that in mind, Swan looks at rolling returns over longer periods—five, ten, or fifteen years. We take into account several investment start and stop dates (because not everyone invests at the same time), as well as different market conditions. Longer rolling periods will generally include a bear market. Therefore, rolling returns over long periods of time provide a more comprehensive view of the consistency of a strategy and the probability of that strategy to deliver a desirable outcome. In contrast, the industry and media at large focus on simple trailing returns over shorter, more recent periods (one, three, or five years), leaving investors to fixate on "beating the market" in the short term. This compounds the emotional behavior that plagues many investors—they switch investments like a frantic driver changing lanes in bumper-to-bumper traffic.

The DRS also redefines asset management. For too long the industry has developed and marketed products that either fit a trend or are easy to deploy, with an emphasis on what's best for the business. I developed the DRS based on what was best for my (the investor's) interest, even if it wasn't necessarily trendy or fit traditional investment classifications.

We know that successful investing does not occur in a cultural vacuum, and history has much to teach us about financial prosperity. A deeper look into recent market history reveals many lessons to learn and questions about changes in the global economy and markets. I hope you find many of the answers you are looking for in *Investing Redefined.*

During my college years, I worked selling self-help books for students on a door-to-door basis. I took the job because I wanted to help others succeed while improving my own ability to share and communicate ideas I knew would advance personal and financial achievement. Maybe some things don't change after all.

Randy Swan
Durango, Colorado
May 2019

I

# THE BIGGER THE CHALLENGE, THE BIGGER THE OPPORTUNITY

"The greatest success stories were created by people who recognized a problem and turned it into an opportunity."
—JOSEPH SUGARMAN

As we near the end of another decade, investors face overwhelming challenges. How can they safely grow their money over the long term with the many risks confronting them? Many in the financial industry claim that traditional strategies are still fine. "No worries," they say. "Keep following the Pied Piper." But their outdated ideas fail to address major threats to investors' wealth, and recent history shows their methods have failed again and again. Those who refuse to challenge or think outside that box may soon regret it.

Many of us face the same daunting question: How do you manage market risk in a low- yield environment? Every investor faces market risk—the chance that markets might sell off by 30 percent, 40 percent, 50 percent, or more. By definition, market risk cannot be diversified away; it can only be hedged.[1] When markets sell off big, strategies based on Modern Portfolio Theory (which is based on diversification through asset allocation) and tactical market timing have failed to grow or protect investors' wealth. The solution I propose has been around for more than two decades. It allows investors to diverge from the failed methods of Wall Street. It doesn't depend on market timing, fundamental analysis, super-skilled stock picking, seemingly random computer algorithms, or deriving safety or return from fixed income (bonds). This solution is a strategy that defines the risk you are willing to take with your wealth and manages it so you don't lose more than you can emotionally or financially handle. It embraces and thrives on challenging investment environments.

Investing, by nature, includes the possibility of market risk, or losing money when broader economic events move the whole market. Yet most investors' approach doesn't allow them to handle this threat well. It took me twenty years to construct my strategy, which I regard as the much-needed solution to the perennial problems of market risk and investors' typical emotional reactions to financial jeopardy. Our answer? A hedged equity approach—the Defined Risk Strategy (DRS).

This strategy does not come from any part of Wall Street nor the stifled thinking that pervades it. Rather, it is the culmination of open-mindedly evaluating investing practices and inserting a mix of professional and personal experiences. I hope to provide help and guidance to the "bottom" 99.5 percent of American investors. The top 0.5 percent has shown they can take care of themselves quite well.

The ideas in this book aim to combat large market declines that can have detrimental, even life-altering impacts on investors' finances and their long-term goals. I want readers to be able to sleep well at night regardless of the effects of world events on the market. It is also, I propose, a possible replacement for (or at the very least an enhancement to) the traditional 60/40 portfolio (60 percent stocks, 40 percent bonds) that many have been implementing for decades. This book is for people who are either investing themselves or have a financial advisor helping them. I assume most readers are familiar with the basics of investing and the various strategies available to them. If you are not, please reference Appendix 2 where I provide some helpful resources to get started. Otherwise, let's keep moving.

This book does not glamorize the investment world or Wall Street. It definitely will not be anything like the many movies or books available on the subject. There are no pop culture icons and no wolves in this story—only wise owls.

## How It All Started

Almost twenty years ago, after ten years in a personal wilderness that required patience, persistence, and dedication, I had a vision. At the time, I ran a modest start-up built around my personal investment strategy, but I dreamed of turning that venture into a robust company that could have a significant impact in the investment world by reaching everyday investors.

I based my approach on the simple idea that it doesn't take genius or secret algorithms to manage market risk, just a logical progression. With the building blocks available, it is possible to solve the quintessential investing problem. In my humble opinion, very few have connected the dots in relation to market risk.

My first realization happened in 1996, thanks to Alan Greenspan, who served as the Federal Reserve chairman at the time. He coined the phrase "irrational exuberance" to describe the stock market during the dot.com bubble and warned that it couldn't last. The market roared on for three and a half years before the bubble finally burst. When it did, I saw that you don't know when it will all go the other way, but it will happen.

I had been saving and investing since my teenage years, but I was still learning. I struggled to decide whether I should ride the market upswings and downturns. In 1996 I concluded that in the current investment environment, traditional solutions like Modern Portfolio Theory (MPT) would not provide normal returns.

Asset allocation methodology claims that the risk of loss can be reduced by diversification, or spreading one's investment dollars over several broad asset classes (e.g., stocks, bonds, cash, and real estate), without a similar reduction in return. The effectiveness of diversification depends on the correlation of those different assets to one another. A positive correlation between two assets (expressed as a number between 0 and 1) means that those two assets move in tandem when the market moves. Conversely, a negative correlation (expressed as a number between 0 and -1) means those two assets move in opposite directions; when one asset goes up in value, the other goes down. A positive correlation of 1.00 means the two assets would move in the exact amount proportionate to one another—if one asset lost 5 percent, the other would also lose 5 percent. A negative correlation of -1.00 would mean if one asset lost 5 percent, the other would gain 5 percent.

This risk reduction from uncorrelated assets is, however, strictly theoretical. It is typically based on relationships that existed over a particular historical period, but there is no guarantee that these relationships or correlations will continue in the future. This is where asset allocation breaks down. Risk is not directly and specifically defined; it is merely expressed in historical standards. The 2008 Financial Crisis disproved these theories when almost all assets became positively correlated, going down together as the market was going down.

### Figure 1.1. Correlation of Major Asset Classes from 1988 to Financial Crisis and during Financial Crisis

Long-Term Correlation Matrix: January 1988 - July 2007

|  | 1 | 2 | 3 | 4 | 5 | 6 |
|---|---|---|---|---|---|---|
| 1) Russell 3000 | 1.00 | 0.62 | 0.61 | 0.52 | 0.41 | -0.08 |
| 2) MSCI EAFE Index | 0.62 | 1.00 | 0.58 | 0.35 | 0.25 | 0.01 |
| 3) MSCI Emerging Markets | 0.61 | 0.58 | 1.00 | 0.43 | 0.30 | 0.04 |
| 4) Barclays U.S. Corp High Yield | 0.52 | 0.35 | 0.43 | 1.00 | 0.44 | -0.11 |
| 5) FTSE Nareit All REITs (Real Estate) | 0.41 | 0.25 | 0.30 | 0.44 | 1.00 | -0.10 |
| 6) S&P GSCI (GS Commodity Index) | -0.08 | 0.01 | 0.04 | -0.11 | -0.10 | 1.00 |

Crisis Correlation Matrix: August 2007 - February 2009

|  | 1 | 2 | 3 | 4 | 5 | 6 |
|---|---|---|---|---|---|---|
| 1) Russell 3000 | 1.00 | 0.92 | 0.83 | 0.75 | 0.86 | 0.59 |
| 2) MSCI EAFE Index | 0.92 | 1.00 | 0.94 | 0.73 | 0.74 | 0.63 |
| 3) MSCI Emerging Markets | 0.83 | 0.94 | 1.00 | 0.75 | 0.62 | 0.69 |
| 4) Barclays U.S. Corp High Yield | 0.75 | 0.73 | 0.75 | 1.00 | 0.70 | 0.50 |
| 5) FTSE Nareit All REITs (Real Estate) | 0.86 | 0.74 | 0.62 | 0.70 | 1.00 | 0.41 |
| 6) S&P GSCI (GS Commodity Index) | 0.59 | 0.63 | 0.69 | 0.50 | 0.41 | 1.00 |

☐ Less than 0.49          ▨ Between 0.80 and 0.89
☐ Between 0.50 and 0.69   ■ Over 0.90
▨ Between 0.70 and 0.79

*Source: Zephyr StyleADVISOR*

As the correlation matrix in Figure 1.1 shows, before the 2008 Crisis, correlations were low between January 1988 and July 2007. So an investor adhering to the asset allocation model would likely believe they were diversified enough to avoid a major loss to their portfolio in a future bear. As you can see in the crisis correlation matrix from August 2007 to February 2009, the correlations went up when investors needed protection the most.

Diversification's success depends on uncorrelated assets, so if you're losing money in one asset, the others should offset the loss. But what if all the assets lose money? Figure 1.2 shows the maximum drawdown each asset class has experienced over the last decade.

### Figure 1.2. Maximum Drawdowns for Major Asset Classes from November 30, 2003 to November 29, 2013

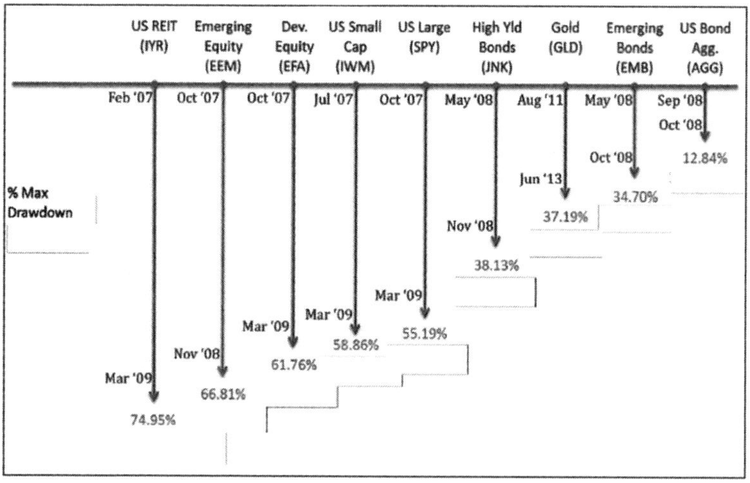

*Source: First Bridge*

While some took a harder hit than others, almost all asset classes went down during the 2008 Crisis.

## The Chessboard Has Changed

Some people may fund retirement through profits, pensions, inheritance, etc. But since most of us cannot accumulate enough money during our working years to sustain a long retirement without the benefit of compounding, everyone needs "normal" investment returns. Through intervention, governments and central banks have permanently changed the investing environment so much that it is no longer conducive to achieving normal investment returns—those necessary for most individuals to reach their personal financial goals. Coupled with that macro shift in policy toward market intervention, increasing globalization presents another important threat to investors. We live in an increasingly interconnected global market system. That means issues abroad can have ramifications at home. The debt woes of countries like Greece threaten to cause impending market fallouts that may impact investors everywhere. Meanwhile, efforts by central banks to prevent those fallouts have unintentionally led to other fallouts.

The chessboard of investing has changed in significant and permanent ways. New players and conditions (central banks, interconnected global markets, etc.)—most of which were not around when the conventional investment philosophy, now prevalent in the industry, was conceived—are now affecting the landscape. Therefore, investors will need to redefine how they consider risk and how they invest going forward.

The US government, together with governments in many other developed countries, has encouraged almost everyone to live beyond their means, sacrificing savers and investors to keep the consumption party going. The Federal Reserve and its central bank cohorts around the globe continue to act in concert as bubble enablers, commenting how they see the long-term problems that exist but insisting it is the politicians that need to fix them. Yet the politicians in both parties seem unwilling to do so. The reality is that it takes both a lender to lend and a borrower to borrow to create the record level of debt that exists today. My guess is that this will not stop. Ever! In fact, there is financial pressure to keep interest rates low as rising rates make debt more expensive, eat into budgets, reduce available funds for services promised, force many investors (pensioners, for example) to accept less than promised, and raise taxes. In the end, everyone wants to say they tried everything, but the laws of nature dictate they will not stop the object already in motion.

Former Chrysler vice chairman Bob Lutz in his book *Guts* compared building a car that a large percentage or majority of people liked but would not buy to building a car that a smaller group would love and also buy. I made a similar strategic decision to move forward against the crowds and against the religion of MPT. We laid everything on the line according to our passion to attract like-minded investors who shared our concerns, who saw first-hand in 2008 and 2009 what happens when systematic risk, or market risk, causes nearly all asset classes to fall in tandem.

My intention is not to appeal to everyone but to demonstrate how the global investing landscape has changed significantly and irreparably, creating challenges that traditional means (diversification, higher taxes, reduced spending, etc.) will not effectively address. It's how the system is set up and it's driven by human nature. I don't wish to prove an economic position. Hundreds of books already outline and discuss the economic problems that exist in greater detail and more convincingly. My sole goal is to show the likelihood of certain impactful global economic events, review the evidence for why the "Smartest Guys in the Room" are at the point of causing a lot of pain for nearly everyone, and show investors what they can do about it. This means redefining how they invest, how they consider risk, and what their portfolio pie looks like to best navigate these challenges and successfully achieve their goals.

## Finding the Solution

As I'm writing, it's been over a decade since the 2008 Crisis and not much has changed in the way investors invest and advisors advise. From my perspective, it's harder for such "defenders of the faith" to challenge the status quo. It's also harder to innovate without some incentive. After all, a lot of money and mental effort goes into creating a business model; it's hard to throw it out the window for a new idea.

I think the same human tendencies account for why no one has considered a solution to market risks such as those I saw brewing in 1996. I looked at the finance industry, government spending and overreach, and the impact of globalization (which is much farther along now than when I first considered developing a new strategy). As an industry outsider, I saw the need for a better way to invest, grow, and protect my wealth. As a worried investor, I had incentive to find a way to withstand those unpredictable but inevitable up and down swings of the markets. I began developing a new approach because I saw the traditional or conventional approaches would not work well going forward in this changing investment landscape (more on why in the next chapter). By 1997 I was ready to implement a strategy I had based on three assumptions:

### 1.  Look Outside the Corner Office and Reject the Status Quo

Why did others not connect the dots or reach the same conclusion? Why did I come up with this solution when no one else did? Was I smarter than everyone else? Although I'm asked these questions frequently, it has always been difficult for me to answer. I did not solve the problem by looking at others' motives, but rather to avoid predisposition, biases, or financial motives. I suspect the solution eluded others due to some or all of the following: groupthink, apathy, laziness, or short-term focus. Others were not focused on risk management at the end of the 1990s when risk actually increased. Because it was easier to keep going down the path of least resistance, very few were focused on what was important: addressing market risk and its detrimental impact on investors' wealth and savings.

Most industries are prone to a certain groupthink or herd mentality. My brother Rob, who worked as an aerospace engineer for a major aircraft manufacturer, recalls how the massive brainpower at his industry-leading company collectively rejected the aerodynamic benefits of winglets. Their engineers defended this position until a small external company scientifically proved the technology's advantages. These same engineers were forced to admit their error and then implement someone else's design. Now most commercial airplanes have winglets to save fuel. You would think that competition would prevent this inertia-causing groupthink, but at some point, people often just accept certain ideas as the way things are, and innovation slows. Insiders may not attempt to solve a problem because they are already getting compensated for what they do. Innovation for its own sake isn't a sufficient motivation. Advocating for change means taking on some career risk if they're wrong.

## 2. Acknowledge Failure

It is often difficult to innovate when you can't or won't admit your own failures. I joke that my "real" graduate degree in finance (as opposed to my master's in professional accounting) was from the school of hard knocks, as I spent years risking my own money while trying various trading strategies. I was fortunate to start investing at age 14, while I was still open to experimentation. By the time I finished college, I had tried many investment techniques and learned what worked and what did not. I managed only my money, so only I suffered when a strategy failed, and I could be honest with myself when something didn't work. At Swan Global Investments, we believe you must first admit that what is traditional or conventional is flawed in order to be open-minded enough to try something new. Otherwise, you will stick with the status quo. It is very difficult to admit failure; it is even harder to change direction.

A successful investment professional rarely has financial incentive to change things. This was especially true in the late 1990s, when both sellers of advice (advisors, broker dealers, financial planners, etc.) and buyers (consumers) believed that you could earn double-digit returns in perpetuity with very little risk. Regardless of how I found a solution to market risk or the reason why others did not, it was bound to happen after the old investment religion (i.e., MPT) was discredited during the 2008 Financial Crisis.

## 3. Acknowledge the Power of Patience

Innovation requires long-term focus, lots of patience, and discipline. There are no shortcuts to investing success. Someone must take the time, energy, and effort (sweat equity) to change the status quo. I've had dozens of people say, "Oh, I've often thought of a strategy like Swan's while raising assets," which I'm sure means there are probably hundreds who share my ideas. But have any of them acted on those thoughts? Actions almost always speak louder than words.

I founded Swan Global Investments in 1997; it took me over twelve years to reach a point where I could live exclusively from its profits. I then spent seven years scaling up to compete in the big leagues. But it was all worth it.

## Are You Ready to Challenge the Status Quo?

In the pages that follow, I will explain how the investment landscape has changed in profound ways to create major problems for investors, why this matters, and what you can do about it.

Chapters 2 and 3 detail how governance and globalization have changed the investment landscape, increasing the very risk and uncertainty they intend to mediate. I examine two recent historical events that demonstrate how the chessboard is changing under investors' feet and what they need to do to be adequately prepared. Chapter 4 explains how Pascal's Wager can be useful in framing a logical decision process to create the right investment philosophy for this new landscape. In Chapter 5, I address the flaws in MPT—the basis for most currently available investment portfolios and investing strategies—as well as why these will not protect investors from future market fallouts and how they create a false sense of security for both investors and advisors. In Chapter 6, I make the case that the typical portfolio needs to look different and offer what I believe is a solution for this. In Chapters 7 and 8, I explain the strategy I employ and how it works, with Chapter 9 presenting how the strategy has weathered various market environments. Chapter 10 lays out the need for investors to challenge the status quo and take matters into their own hands because no one else will.

2

# WHEN THE SMARTEST GUYS IN THE ROOM FAIL: GOVERNMENT, DEBT, AND NATURAL LAW

Just as investors have been let down and led astray by the industry "defenders of the faith" who cling to the traditional methods of Modern Portfolio Theory (MPT), they have also put their faith in another misguided group of insiders. I call them the Smartest Guys in the Room. These are the officials, academics, politicians, and government experts who set the financial policy for our nation and around the world. Ostensibly the brightest, best educated, and best equipped to confront our financial issues, these people ignore, in my opinion, the most basic principles that govern the markets, wealth management, and fiscal growth: natural law.

Natural law can refer to either observable laws relating to natural phenomena or a body of unchanging moral principles—what goes up, must go down; for every force, there is an opposing force; people primarily seek their self-interests; people have a self-preservation instinct, just to name a few. While the concept of natural law is typically associated with philosophy, it also matters in discussions of theoretical economics.[1] In the physical and mathematical world, natural law determines what and how natural events will occur. In the moral world, it determines unchanging human rights and responsibilities. Natural law posits that there are inherent laws or truths that guide and explain human behavior regardless of whatever manmade laws there may be. Humans will act how they will act regardless of the "rules." Natural law preexists courts, judges, legislative bodies, executives, and regulators.

It is critical for investors to understand the importance of basic universal principles, which, if not followed, will result in an environment that is less than ideal for prosperity at best, and at worst, will render disastrous results (think about the collapse of the Soviet Union, recent problems in Greece, and the disintegration of Venezuela in 2016–17). Ignoring these principles is not without impact. Degrees of change may result in minimizing some of the damage, but even lightly ignoring these principles will reduce prosperity, and over time, will put you between the proverbial rock and a hard place. The road to destruction is a long one and takes time to reach its ultimate conclusion. Paraphrasing Ernest Hemingway in *The Sun Also Rises*, the way a country goes broke is slowly at first and then suddenly.

## The Smartest Guys Are Failing

The Smartest Guys in the Room (SGRs), especially those in our government, have been fighting against natural law for a while now. Through their decisions, government has overstepped its power and acted against reasonable, naturally derived principles of ethics and economics. They have created, I believe, adverse economic conditions that make it challenging for investors to manage their investments and wealth, and ultimately their futures. Unsustainable spending and interventionist policies affect investors at every step of their investment journey, from how much money they have to save and invest to how they are going to invest, to how their gains are taxed, to how well their money will be protected in a shaky economy or turbulent market.

For evidence that the SGRs ignore natural economic law, we need look no further than the following:

- Out-of-control government spending (including waste, fraud, and abuse)

- Federal Reserve intervention
- Foreign central bank activity (easy money messing with the natural business cycles of economies, coupled with artificially low interest rates)
- Improper incentives
- Increasing taxes, which de-incentivize work, production, and wealth creation

These are just a few examples of the ways government smart guys interfere with natural law by ignoring or even actively undermining universal principles. Pushing easy money or keeping interest rates too low for too long violates free market principles. This can lead to an eventual consequence—and often not a pleasant one. Among other things, this interference has created the current environment in which the government tries to fix the perceived problem of decreased aggregate demand. The SGRs, central bankers, politicians, and heads of Wall Street fear deflation more than anything else, so they have artificially lowered rates and kept them low to induce more demand. This intervention has resulted in the current bond situation, where long-term bond yields are almost as low as short-term bond yields, discouraging saving and bond investment and setting up a major interest rate risk going forward. This bond situation, in turn, puts more pressure on investors to find returns elsewhere (either higher yield, riskier bonds, or in the volatile, highly valued stock market) to get the desired return from their portfolios. This Keynesian approach of increased government expenditures and intervention adopted by the SGRs not only goes against the history of markets, but also relies on manipulating the markets to do something contrary to their long-term best interests.

We are beginning to suffer the consequences of violating these natural principles, starting with the markets and cascading into our investing strategies and financial plans. Despite numerous warnings from many sources, the SGRs seem determined to push every major economic or social problem into the future, from the solvency and sustainability of Social Security, Medicare, and Medicaid to the national debt and budget deficits, to monetary policy and more. Politicians from both sides in Washington, D.C., continually kick the can farther down the road and increase the potential for disastrous effects on our financial future.

Let's look at some of their greatest missteps.

## Government Debt

Very few would argue that the United States does not have a debt problem. It is very obvious and frustrating to most that our government is unconcerned or unable to solve it. Government debt threatens to eat into everyone's financial futures. As long as lenders have a financial stake in loans they originate, there is a natural limit to what individuals can borrow and service, and what lenders will lend. Yet that simple economic principle seems to escape our SGRs. How can they not see that debt eats future growth? Every dollar borrowed today requires forgoing one dollar of future consumption plus the interest paid on that borrowed dollar. So instead of a dollar being used to consume goods and services, that dollar plus interest is spent instead in debt payments, thereby slowing economic growth. The US economy is primarily a consumer-driven economy—dollars not spent on consumption hurts gross domestic product (GDP), and that goes for consumers as well as governments.

Statistics show that our nation's monetary policy—the controlling of interest rates and the money supply by the Federal Reserve—has had little or no impact on the mainstream economy or population. The primary effect has been a bloated stock market, which is both the only game in town and nearing all-time highs, setting up a perfect storm. Traditional, balanced portfolio approaches to investing (a mix of stocks and bonds) will likely be unable to deliver historic expectations in terms of performance, as bond yields are low and bond values will be eroded by any future rise in the currently low interest rates. I expand more on the plight of bonds and the balanced portfolio in Chapter 5. It is also very unlikely that bonds, or fixed-income investments will continue to be effective as a safe haven in future bear markets. Mainstream investors will likely suffer most in this scenario set up by the SGRs. Statistically speaking, that's probably you.

In *The Wall Street Journal* in 2012, Lawrence Goodman, former US Treasury official and head of the Center for Financial Stability, wrote:

The Fed is in effect subsidizing U.S. government spending and borrowing via expansion of its balance sheet and massive purchases of Treasury bonds. This keeps Treasury interest rates abnormally low, camouflaging the true size of the budget deficit . . . The failure by officials to normalize conditions in the U.S. Treasury market and curtail ballooning deficits puts the U.S. economy and markets at risk for a sharp correction.[2]

So, if and when rates rise, the cost of servicing (making the payments for) that national debt will grow, making it more and more costly to pay off as interest rates rise. It's like digging a big hole of credit card debt.

Figure 2.1 shows the growth of the national debt since 1900. Note that virtually all of the debt was created after 1913, when the Federal Reserve and income tax debuted in our economy, which I believe created an imbalance that has set us on the road to perdition.

## Figure 2.1. Real Federal Debt with Estimates to 2018 (Log Scale)

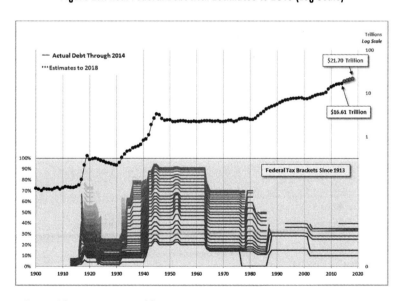

*Source: Advisor Perspectives; dshort.com*

A similar chart, Figure 2.2, displays a noticeable shift in the size and growth rate of the national debt since 1970. All this time, both political parties have been culpable, each side too busy engaging in cronyism and fixing blame on the opposing party to be bothered with addressing our nation's debt burden.

────────────────── **Figure 2.2. Federal Debt** ──────────────────

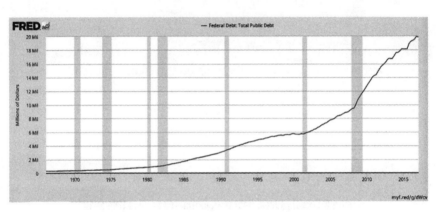

*Source: US Department of the Treasury, Fiscal Service; fred.stlouisfed.org*

────── **Figure 2.3. Historical and Estimated Deficits of Federal Budget** ──────

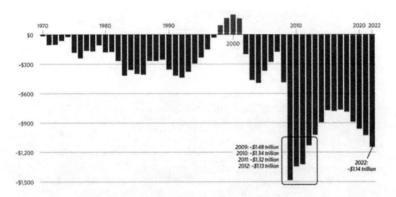

*Sources: Office of Management and Budget, Budget of the US Government, FY 2013: Historical Tables, Table 1.1, February 2012, http://www.whitehouse.gov/omb/budget/Historicals (accessed August 8, 2012), and Congressional Budget Office, An Update to the Budget and Economic Outlook: Fiscal Years 2012 to 2022, Alternative Fiscal Scenario, August 22, 2012, http://cbo.gov/publication/43543 (accessed August 23, 2012).*

More worrisome, this trend seems global: From 2007 to 2015, around $57 trillion of debt was added worldwide.

## Figure 2.4. Global Debt Since the Great Recession

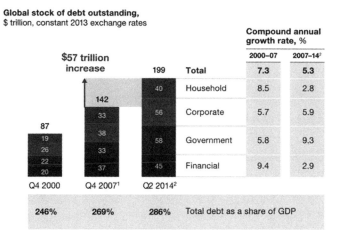

**Since the Great Recession, global debt has increased by $57 trillion, outpacing world GDP growth.**

Global stock of debt outstanding, $ trillion, constant 2013 exchange rates

| | Compound annual growth rate, % | |
|---|---|---|
| | 2000–07 | 2007–14[2] |
| Total | 7.3 | 5.3 |
| Household | 8.5 | 2.8 |
| Corporate | 5.7 | 5.9 |
| Government | 5.8 | 9.3 |
| Financial | 9.4 | 2.9 |

| Q4 2000 | Q4 2007[1] | Q2 2014[2] | Total debt as a share of GDP |
|---|---|---|---|
| 246% | 269% | 286% | |

*Source: Bank for International Settlements; Haver Analytics: International Monetary Fund World Economic Outlook; national sources; McKinsey Global Institute analysis.*

This new debt equates to approximately $77.4 million per day since the birth of Christ in 1 AD, a period of more than 736,000 days.

## Unfunded Liabilities

At Swan, we often refer to an old *Saturday Night Live* skit whereby a character played by Chris Parnell tries to explain his new program to help people get out of debt.[3] It would be even more hilarious if it were not so true. Parnell promotes his simple solution, a book titled *Don't Buy Stuff You Cannot Afford*. His clients, Steve Martin and Amy Poehler, cannot wrap their heads around the concept of only buying things they can actually afford. No matter the scenario presented, the consumers (Steve and Amy) want to borrow the money to make the purchase and spend more than they have.

Like SNL's Poehler and Martin in the sketch, the federal government has total unfunded liabilities (future payments promised, but for which there is no money) for entitlement programs such as Social Security, Medicare, and Medicaid in the amount of $107 trillion.[4] Based on current laws, the present net value of future liabilities owed by our government equates to approximately $890K per taxpayer. Do you have $890K lying around? Do you want it going to the government?

The alternative fiscal scenario (AFS) of the Congressional Budget Office (CBO) lists $205 trillion in unfunded legal liabilities (compared to the $47 trillion stated on its much more publicized extended baseline forecast). According to Laurence Kotlikoff, economics professor at Boston University:

> The $205 trillion fiscal gap is enormous. It's 10 percent of the present value of all future GDP. Equivalently, it corresponds to 10 percent of GDP year in and year out for as far as the eye can see. To raise 10 percent of GDP each year we could (a) raise all federal taxes, immediately and permanently, by 57 percent, (b) cut all federal spending, apart from interest on the debt, by 37 percent, immediately and permanently, or (c) do some combination of (a) and (b).[5]

Not very likely. University of Pennsylvania Wharton School finance professor Robert Inman has also spoken frankly about the issue. A 2015 Wharton blog included his comments from a Penn Institute for Urban Research conference on the financial health of cities: "Inman provided this cautionary perspective: 'This is a serious problem, and there is no running away from it. It has made the front pages of every financial newspaper in the world, and rightly so.' He noted that researchers who have studied this crisis have 'corrected a fundamental flaw in the way that people were thinking about these unfunded liabilities.' The bottom line, Inman said, was that there were $3 trillion worth of unfunded pension liabilities at the state level and $400 billion of unfunded liabilities at the large-city level. That turns out to be about $10,000 per American citizen."[6]

Rationally, investors must come to a clear conclusion about this debt problem. It is not sustainable and something has to give. At some point the outcome of this indebtedness is all or some combination of the following: government expenditures or services will be reduced, taxes will be raised, and pensioners and government debtors will be forced to accept less than expected.

The same SGRs that created this debt supercycle will be forced to make very hard choices to deal with the consequences of decline in the aggregate demand. The forced decisions will cause long-term investors great pain; their nest eggs will suffer enormous damage. Of course, the sooner we recognize there is a problem and make the necessary adjustments, the easier and less painful the solution will be.

In summary, the total federal, state, and local debt (including unfunded liabilities) is around $107 trillion (or $204 trillion if you go by the CBO's alternative fiscal scenario). This debt increases each and every year and is expected to accelerate at a faster rate in the future. Our accelerated debt problem is further exacerbated by an almost unlimited desire to offer more spending, more programs, and more free stuff in the hopes of gaining unlimited and unchecked power. As we are seeing in Greece and Venezuela, the laws of nature demand that it will end; it is just a matter of when, not if.

## State and Local Pensions

State and local pensions are also headed for a cliff. Unlike the federal government where the Federal Reserve can control the currency, state and local governments do not permit unlimited borrowing. States have borrowed lots of money, but their biggest problem is their collective unfunded pension liabilities for their employees. Votes have been effectively bought by promising overly generous pension benefits. The following chart (Figure 2.5) shows this trend in the gap between assets and unfunded liabilities.

## Figure 2.5. Tracking State Pension Assets and Liabilities, FY 1997-2015

Gap increased in 2015, the second year of new reporting standards

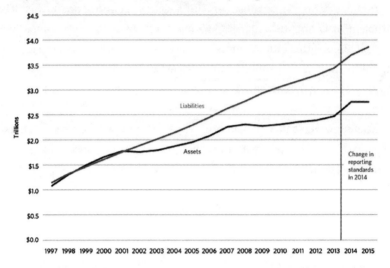

*Source: Comprehensive annual financial reports, actuarial reports and valuations, or other public documents, or as provided by plan officials ©The Pew Charitable Trusts*

A recent *Wall Street Journal* piece titled "The Hidden Danger in Public Pension Funds" stated, "The ratio of active public employees to retirees has fallen drastically, according to the State Budget Crisis Task Force. Today it is 1.75 to 1; in 1950, it was 7 to 1. This means that a loss in pension investments has three times the impact on state and local budgets than 40 years ago."[7] The funding gap is not just a problem due to overly generous pension benefits, but an underfunding of defined benefit plans with fewer workers paying into the pension coffers versus the number of retirees taking funds out, as well as incorrect assumptions for returns (most pension plans assume a 7 percent to 8 percent long-term return).

California is a prime example of this mismanagement. According to a Bloomberg study, a state prison psychiatrist was paid $822K, a highway patrol officer collected $484K in pay and pension benefits, and seventeen employees received checks of more than $200K for unused vacation and leave . . . Unions persuaded the California Public Employees' Retirement

System to sponsor legislation, called Senate Bill 400, which sweetened state and local pensions and gave retroactive increases for tens of thousands of retirees. Highway-patrol officers were granted the right to retire after thirty years of service with 90 percent of their top salaries, a benefit that was copied by police agencies across the state.

Some cities that adopted the highway-patrol pension plan later cited those costs for contributing to their bankruptcy filings. According to Bloomberg, "California had almost 11,000 workers in the Department of Corrections and Rehabilitation who made $100,000 or more in 2011, and about 900 prison employees earning more than $200,000 a year . . . New York had none. Its top-paid officer is a sergeant at Sing Sing Correctional Facility who made $170,000 last year."[8] This is not to say these jobs aren't dangerous or worth a certain amount of pay, but government sector pay and benefits have gotten way out of line, creating a new higher standard or precedent for salaries and pensions.

Here are a few other outrageous examples:

- A governor's chauffeur who worked his way up to deputy public safety commissioner and then state director of homeland security retired at forty-eight and received a retroactive payment of $177,000 and an annual pension payment of $94,000.[9]

- According to the *Arizona Republic* in 2015, some Arizona retirees could expect to earn more within a few years of retirement than they earned while working full-time for the government (and the pension plan is only 67 percent funded).[10]

- Lifeguards in New Jersey (four months of beach season) after twenty years of service can retire at forty-five and qualify for pensions equal to half their salary. The laws that set this up haven't changed since 1936.[11]

## Demographics Is Destiny

One of the main reasons for the debt problem is that US demographic distribution no longer supports current and future retirees. The ongoing decline in the number of workers supporting retirees will not make things any easier. The math is flawed; people are now living longer than when pensions were conceived, so there are too many retirees relative to workers paying current benefits. It is the classic definition of a Ponzi scheme: Today's investors pay for yesterday's, as opposed to each retiree funding their own retirement.

Demographics are not just a US problem, but a global one. By 2030, fifty-six countries will have more people aged sixty-five and over than children under fifteen, according to a recent Bloomberg study.

——————— Figure 2.6. Estimates of the U.S. Population, by Age, 1950 to 2050 ———————

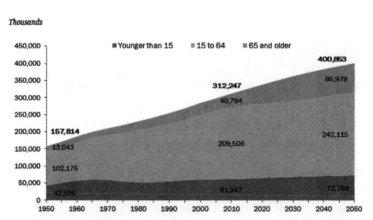

Source: United Nations, Department of Economic and Social Affairs, *World Population Prospects: 2012 Revision*, June 2013, http://esa.un.org/unpd/wpp/index.htm

**PEW RESEARCH CENTER**

*Source: United Nations, Department of Economic and Social Affairs, World Population Prospects: 2012 Revision, June 2013, http://esa.un.org/unpd/wpp/index.htm. Pew Research Center.*

The US population is aging, and we are not currently having enough children to replace the adult working population. A prosperous economy

requires an increasing population lest it stagnate. Immigration helps but
has numerous side effects when not properly managed: challenges with
assimilation, successful integration into the economy, and government's
ability to manage disparate needs/customs of its citizenry.

## — Figure 2.7. Social Security–Workers per Beneficiary (Historical and Estimated) —

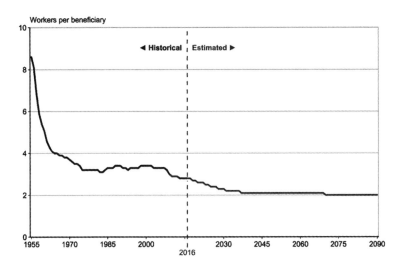

*Source: Social Security Administration; ssa.gov*

Something has to give. Expenditures will, most assuredly, get reduced
at some point but not before enormous damage is done to the US economy. The effects of these demographic pressures are already being felt by
the low growth rate our economy has experienced since the 2008 Financial Crisis.

— Figure 2.8. Entitlement Spending as Pct Government US from FY 1900 to FY 2020 —

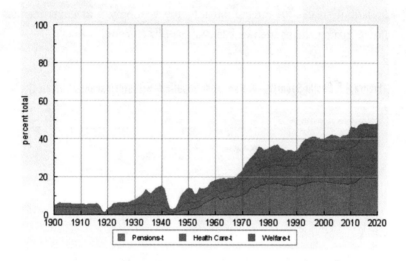

Source: usgovernmentspending.com

There's a lot of truth in the common phrase "demographics is destiny"—a relevant observation for our times. As so much government spending is earmarked for entitlements, and with an expanding and aging population, there is little hope that this borrow and spend approach will stop any time soon. Unfortunately, as interest rates rise, more and more of the government's budget will be spent on obligations (entitlements) and interest payments for the national debt, while less and less can be put toward services. Then a raise in revenues (taxes) will be deemed necessary. This cycle becomes more vicious as interest rates move higher and the government piles on more debt. The effect is essentially theft from our children and grandchildren in that we have incurred so much debt that it will be forced upon their generations. Their quality of life will likely decline. As noted earlier, the laws of nature demand that it will end; it is just a matter of when, not if.

## Drowning in the Deep End of the Debt Pool

The American economy is rife with warnings of danger. As former Federal Reserve chair Alan Greenspan stated on CNBC in 2014: "The Fed's balance sheet is a pile of tinder, but it hasn't been lit . . . inflation will eventually have to rise." Former US Treasury official John Kitchen and economics professor Menzie Chinn of the University of Wisconsin published a study in 2010 titled "Financing U.S. Debt: Is There Enough Money in the World—and at What Cost?" The journalist Mark Steyn refers to this study in his book, *After America*, writing:

> The fact that sane men are even asking this question ought to be deeply disturbing. As to the answer, foreign official holdings of U.S. Treasury securities have usually been less than 5 percent of the rest of the world's GDP. By 2009, they were up to 7 percent. By 2020, Kitchen and Chinn project them to rise to about 19 percent of the rest of the world's GDP, which they say is . . . *do-able*. Whether the rest of the world will want to do it is another matter. A future that presumes the rest of the planet will sink a fifth of its GDP into U.S. Treasuries is no future at all.[12]

All of this debt will have cascading ramifications for investors. Large debt loads create pressure on governments to keep rates low, cut spending, or raise taxes. Low rates hurt bond investors and thus puts undue pressure on the traditional balanced approach to portfolio asset allocation. Reduced spending will cause an economic slowdown and stock market hit, thereby hitting investors either directly in areas of employment or indirectly in their investments. Higher taxes will eat investor returns and diminish realized income. Thus, investors need to understand these likely outcomes, assess the risks, and redefine how they invest going forward.

## Taxes—No Panacea Indeed

What really shocks me is that this debt persists despite ongoing collection of federal taxes. But in the end, politicians will always spend more than the government takes in. History has proven that time and time again. From political candidates we hear no end of promises: free preschool and college, "shovel-ready" jobs on infrastructure projects, mandatory or even guaranteed higher wages, free health care, and increased military spending. So the budget deficits grow, as does the national debt.

In 2014, economic policy analyst Stephen Moore wrote in *The Washington Post*: "In a globally competitive world, jobs, capital, and wealth tend to migrate from high- to low-tax locations."[13] This is a universal truth. It is a fallacy to assume that the ultra-wealthy are going to pay or should pay for the government waste, fraud, and abuse (including wealth redistribution) that are rampant in our system. This scenario is even more unlikely or even impossible when considering the small size of the pool of the truly rich. According to the 2010 US Census, 325 million people were living in 160 million households, so that's only 1.6 million households in the United States in the top 1 percent.[14] The average pretax income of these households in the top 1 percent is about $2.1 million.[15] If you took all of that income, $2.1 million multiplied by 1.6 million homes, that's about $3.36 trillion dollars. The national debt as of August 2018 is well over $21 trillion and rising each day.[16] Plus the federal budget is projected to increase another 31 percent in just five years, with spending increasing from $3.9 trillion in 2016 to $5.1 trillion in 2021.[17] There simply isn't enough money at the top 1 percent to cover our fiscal problems, even if fully confiscated. Even if that top 1 percent had their *entire* net worth somehow liquidated and handed over to the government, it would only knock off about one-third of the $21-plus trillion national debt. The economic impact and amount of jobs lost on a 100 percent tax is practically unfathomable. You can only kill the golden goose once.

OK, so taxing the wealthy at 100 percent is not reasonable. What if we just raise their tax rates? What will that do for our annual budget deficits? It is important to note that the Office of Management and Budget (OMB) forecasts a deficit of at least $450–$500 billion a year through fiscal year 2024. Fiscal year 2017 saw a budget deficit of $666 billion.[18]

A 2015 study from the liberal-leaning Tax Policy Center also shows important data related to the top 1 percent. The top 1 percent's average annual income comes in around $2.1 million and their average tax rate has been about one-third of that or 33.4 percent. For this example, let's assume the entire top 1 percent has to pay twice as much in taxes, or 66.8 percent. If these individuals do not take drastic steps to reduce this tax burden (not reasonable) or if they simply move out of the United States to lower tax jurisdictions (more likely), we could raise tax revenues by about $793 billion. The $793 billion would cover the OMB's estimated budget deficit ($500 billion per year) and contribute to paying down our $19.97 trillion national debt. However, at this rate, it would take a whopping sixty-eight years to pay off our national debt assuming no adverse effect of this onerous tax rate on the US economy (and also assuming no change or increase in government debt or annual deficits).

More likely and with much greater impact, the middle and upper-middle class will have to pay for the largest portion of our debt burden. Lack of knowledge and lack of holding elected officials accountable for their decisions and actions are no excuse. Are we electing the government we deserve? Grover G. Norquist, president of Americans for Tax Reform, said, "Taxation is not charity. It is not voluntary. As we shrink the state and make government smaller, we will find that more and more people are able to take care of themselves."[19]

Government, by its nature, grows. And by its nature, government is not efficient in its collection and allocation of resources. While the private sector generally rewards efficiency, the public sector often rewards inefficiency. Government departments or programs are not rewarded with larger budgets if they find efficient ways to execute their roles or tasks using less of an allocated budget. In fact, in such instances, unused budgets simply mean a smaller budget the following year. Thus, as government grows, more funds are required to execute its role, however inefficient that execution may be.

Human nature is constant and observable, and over time, patterns can be seen. The pattern I've outlined of government overreach, overspending, and debt accumulation was not what this nation's Founding Fathers intended. In fact, they sought to prevent it, having witnessed the propensity for those in power (governments of many forms) to take advantage of the many to benefit the few. Having the benefit of hindsight, they assessed and discussed previous democracies and why they failed in the past, including the Greek and Roman empires, and purposefully set up a democratic republic with a framework that provided the best possible chance for long-term success, taking human nature into account.

The so-called American experiment was based on a distinct framework that deliberately constrained government power and growth. The Constitution expressly enumerated the government's powers and clearly stated that the people retain all authority. Doing this maximized individual liberty. Not only does our founding framework define and limit the federal government's powers, but the Founding Fathers saw the need to split up those federal powers within separate yet equal branches or departments with checks and balances to further limit the temptation to accumulate power. In "Federalist No. 51," James Madison (or Alexander Hamilton)[20] wrote extensively on the necessity to create checks and balances, famously asserting, "If men were angels, no government would be necessary." The idea of limited government was central to the founding of these United States of America. To the degree that we have allowed, slowly and progressively over time, the federal government, and to varying degrees state governments, to grow and accumulate powers outside of that box, we have sown the seeds of excess and cronyism that have grown unchecked.

Nonetheless, the disregard of these limitations on government power is yet another example of what happens when you let politicians and judges supersede the Constitution. It is apparent that it is just another violation of the natural laws that will ultimately have devastating consequences since it upsets the natural balance.

When will this government overreach and overspending stop? Obviously, the government will continue to spend well beyond its means regardless of who is in power and how much tax they collect. The pattern of taxation and spending, without natural constraints, will continue unabated until the natural limits are eventually reached. Prior to the tax and spend endgame, the system becomes progressively more unjust, corrupt, and unsustainable. The fact is we simply can't tax our way out of this dilemma. As a reminder, some of the consequences of rising debt include lower income, pressure for larger tax increases and spending cuts, reduced ability to respond to unexpected events, and an ever-greater chance of fiscal crisis. Thus, the ramifications of a growing debt problem and the resulting tax increases will spread to investors one way or another.

Besides leveraging the power individuals have with the voting booth and civic activism to change those in power and thereby change the course we're on, logic dictates that investors should pursue investment strategies that are tax-efficient.

## Aggregate Demand

It's hard to predict the impact of government spending cuts on the market, US economy, or global economies. Given that the Federal Reserve and central bankers around the globe are doing everything possible to avoid or delay the inevitable, we believe the impact will not be easy or painless. As an analogy, the government used to try to prevent all forest fires. Then research found that regular, smaller fires regulate overgrowth, help prevent larger fires, and help regenerate forests.

The SGRs are making the same mistake in preventing all "fires" in the market. Their efforts to prevent any decline also keep any steam from escaping. With no outlet for this build up of pressure, the natural law of economics will eventually cause the situation to burst, much like the natural laws of physics would do to a kettle under pressure. When things do blow up economically, we are likely due for a much larger and painful experience.

Again, by definition, debt robs future consumption. Therefore, incurring too much debt robs growth—more than we'd like to sacrifice. Consider Japan, which has been in a downward spiral since the late 1980s (when many believed their business model, based largely on leverage and borrowing against over-valued, debt-backed securities, would rule the world). Now, they have the oldest average population and one of the lowest birth rates in the world, and the highest percentage of debt to GDP of any developed nation. Are the economic struggles of debt and demographics of the last few decades a coincidence? I think not.

Many other countries, such as Greece, Argentina, Venezuela, Ukraine, Belarus, and Jamaica, are not far behind Japan or are headed in the same direction. Developed nations are in the proverbial rock and a hard place now. How will this global debt bubble play out?

## Likely Economic Outcome

The government likely will reach first into the pockets of the truly rich (top 0.5 percent). When they've taken all they can there, the SGRs will then move down to the 1 percent, then the top 5 percent, and so on. We've already shown that there isn't enough money there, so eventually the tax burden will hit the middle class. As there will not be enough money to satisfy existing obligations, the SGRs will require debt restructuring or benefit cuts.

Let's estimate conservatively, say a one-third cut in entitlements. Then, everyone relying on a government pension—and most of those dependent on private pensions—will be forced to live on two-thirds or less of what they were expecting. These losses are likely to be compounded by losses in our financial markets. This scenario will be difficult, if not impossible, since most individuals have very little in savings (approximately $63,000) beyond their retirement plans.[21] The loss of savings and income will have devastating effects on the whole economy, directly translating to a one-third loss in consumer spending throughout the country. As consumers account for 64 percent of our $18 trillion GDP, this will be comparable to losing $3.8 trillion from our economy. If you think we have problems now with low growth, you haven't seen anything yet.

Companies providing goods and services to the government will also see their revenues instantly cut when government spending decreases. The changes they make to personnel, compensation, and so on will bleed into the rest of the economy, affecting private and public companies alike. The loss of trust in the government and our economic system, along with fallout from the fleecing of productive people of all socioeconomic classes, will create further economic and market ripples.

# The Chief Enablers–Postponing the Day of Reckoning

If a reckoning is a matter of when and not if, why hasn't it happened yet? With all of these disastrous spending habits and overwhelming debt, it is fair to ask, "What's keeping the party going?"

The Federal Reserve and world central banks continue to intervene and prop things up. A study conducted at the University of Missouri–Kansas City assessed the total size of the Fed's commitments—asset purchases as well as loans—and found that the Federal Reserve bailout commitment exceeds $29 trillion.[22]

Our country's banking history has had its (very) rough patches. Prior to the 1913 establishment of the Federal Reserve, all other attempts at a national bank had failed. The US banking system was a giant mess of small, local, unregulated banks tied to local economies. Whenever a local economy slowed and struggled, so did the local banks. By the 1920s, the United States had nearly 30,000 banks, more than the rest of the world put together. The Fed was reorganized during the Great Depression and again in the 1960s. Finally, in the 1990s, interstate banking was allowed, and giant nationwide banks began to form and grow, touting benefits like convenience and economies of scale. We saw some of the drawbacks, however, during the 2008 Financial Crisis when the Fed had to bail many of them out as they were deemed "too big to fail."

Now, the powerful Federal Reserve has established control over the national economy and the banking system. Its supporters likely believe that with our incredible technology and involvement by the SGRs, our central bank cannot fail. History proves otherwise. There has been a financial panic or banking crisis in the United States roughly every twenty years since the Fed was founded. Despite history's lessons about the danger of centralization, the Fed has so much power over the markets and economy that it seemingly can manipulate and affect growth and employment at will. While it may have kept the party going over the last decade (market growth), natural law will eventually prevail.

The Federal Reserve states its purpose as:

- Conducting the nation's monetary policy by influencing money and credit conditions in the economy in pursuit of full employment and stable prices.

- Supervising and regulating banks and other important financial institutions to ensure the safety and soundness of the nation's banking and financial system and to protect the credit rights of consumers.

- Maintaining the stability of the financial system and containing systemic risk that may arise in financial markets.

- Providing certain financial services to the U.S. government, U.S. financial institutions, and foreign official institutions, and playing a major role in operating and overseeing the nation's payments systems.[23]

We commonly hear the Fed say things like: "We raised interest rates to cool down rampant inflation," or "We lowered interest rates to stimulate growth and investment and to get the economy moving again." Where does the money go when the Fed makes its decisions? To the public? No. To the banks, either directly or indirectly. At its core, the Fed is just a banking cartel, and its sole purpose is to keep the banks afloat and keep the spending party going. Other central banks around the world have followed suit. This rampant loose monetary policy will eventually come home to roost.

Reflecting on its management of the Great Depression; recessions in the 1950s, '60s, '70s, and '80s; the tech bubble (and burst); and the 2008 Financial Crisis, the Fed hasn't exactly painted a very good picture of economic stability throughout its history. You don't have to be a rocket scientist to figure out what the endgame will be: The Fed will introduce a "stealth" tax on all Americans via inflation. Make no mistake; there will eventually be a reckoning. Such reckless policies will likely magnify its effects.

As stated, the purpose of the Fed is to supervise and regulate the economy through monetary policy to ensure stability of the financial system. I argue that it has strayed far from this mission, instead rewarding bad habits by the banks, and by doing so, sowing the seeds for a future financial crisis. If we examine the two most recent bear markets (2000 and 2008), we can see that our global leaders didn't really learn from history. Nor should we expect them to—ever. Human nature dooms us to repeat mistakes especially when we are insulated from their consequences—and sometimes even when we have to pay a price.

The economic and social problems that plagued past decades still exist today. In some cases, they've even become worse. In the last nine years, the poor have gotten poorer, the rich have gotten richer, and the middle class has gotten stuck. The government's solution of tax and spend cannot fix the problems it helped create.

## The Bottom Line

The rich are not going to save us. There are only 16,000 super wealthy families (those in the top 0.01 percent) in the country with a net worth of at least $111 million (when studied in 2012).[24] The debt problem is too big. In fact, there is not enough money (more than $90 trillion as of 2017, including all coins, banknotes, money market accounts, savings, checking, and time deposits) in all of the world to pay for the global debt in developed markets (more than $215 trillion, including government, corporate, and household debt).[25] We cannot tax or seize our way out of this situation. Further, wealth does not form in countries where property rights are not respected, and taxes are an aspect of property. In the current imperfect tax system, the truly rich (1 percent and above) will hire those who are smarter than the politicians, or they will leave. While it may make some people feel better to imagine others paying the bill for their "free stuff," there is simply not enough in the 1 percent to pay for our debt. While the concept of higher taxes for the few may be voted on by the many, it will ultimately fall on the shoulders of the many, not the few.

As a student of history, I prefer to learn from the Smartest Guys' mistakes, even if they will not. I believe an investor's best chance at personally avoiding this disaster is to look at the past for clues to how these situations ultimately played out.

# 3

# WHEN THE LEVEE BREAKS &
# THOSE YOU TRUST FAIL YOU:
# LESSONS FROM RECENT HISTORY

The study of history and the natural rhythms of world societies is necessary for designing a strategy for all seasons. I can think of no time in history where the laws of nature did not ultimately correct excesses of spending and liabilities such as those we see today. Does this mean something bad is just around the corner? Not necessarily, but given that the government did not follow the drastic steps necessary to achieve temporary stabilization in 2008 with meaningful changes in policy, our chances are much higher. No matter the catalyst for each painful bubble bursting—whether overvalued stocks, real estate prices, or negative yielding government bonds—the root causes have not been resolved.

The housing crisis, for example, was predicated on choices made more than two decades prior to the ultimate collapse. Yet our leaders never truly took responsibility for their actions: encouraging the expansion of credit through rhetoric and changes in the law, spurring risky borrowing through the rapid and steep lowering of interest rates, and initiating bailouts with public funds (our tax dollars) after the collapse. Such actions effectively set up a system of moral hazard.

Moral hazard occurs when one person takes more risks because someone else bears the cost of those risks. Originators make decisions knowing another party will bear the costs if things go badly. The party isolated from the risk behaves differently than they would if fully exposed to the risk.

I suspect some could argue that the 2007–09 crisis came out of the same bubble that was reflated after the dot.com collapse in 2000–02. But whether overvalued stocks, real estate prices, or negative yielding government bonds cause a bubble doesn't matter. The problems have not been resolved. The Smartest Guys in the Room (SGRs) are still happily in the business of creating bubbles. Collectively, we should have learned from these mistakes. My takeaway is that government will stop at nothing to save the day and is all-in trying to stop the inevitable.

The government has created this environment through its handling of previous crises. Let's take a look at the Long-Term Capital Management (LTCM) crisis in 1998 and how it laid the groundwork for both the dot.com bust and the 2008 Crisis. With no significant behavior or policy changes, and ongoing expectations that the Fed will continue bailing out the banks, what's stopping a future bubble and subsequent collapse? Two of my favorite financial books, *When Genius Failed* and *The Big Short*, highlight some of the lessons we should have learned from 1998 to 2007–09.

## Sowing the Seeds

*When Genius Failed* was published in 2000 by Roger Lowenstein and is an account of the rise and fall of a hedge fund manager, Long-Term Capital Management. LTCM's story demonstrates the consequences of refusing to let natural law take its course, pushing the problem to the future, and thereby creating a larger problem. According to Lowenstein, the ultimate failure of LTCM jeopardized not only some of the largest banks in the United States, but also the financial stability of the global financial system itself. So much so, that the Federal Reserve had to get involved, coordinating a bank-wide $3.6 billion bailout to restore stability in the financial markets.[1]

Back in the late '90s, many hailed LTCM's Long-Term Capital Portfolio as the most impressive hedge fund in history, mostly because of the individuals involved in its founding (the types everyone would consider the

Smartest Guys in the Smartest Room): a notoriously successful bond arbitrageur, two Nobel Prize-winning economists, and many Wall Street and academia elites. LTCM was considered one of the best money managers in the world, and it appeared to be so for several years. Their hedge fund grew at a steady pace for years before suffering an 80 percent loss within five weeks when Russia defaulted on its domestic bonds. LTCM didn't account for this possibility and clearly suffered for it.

LTCM incorporated a lot of leverage in its strategy, borrowing money to make more money to pay back the initial loan while still retaining profits. A great idea in theory, it works well if everything goes as expected. But the one time it doesn't, and you can't pay back what you owe, you're in big trouble.

Here are some of the blind spots or miscalculations of LTCM's principals:

1. **LTCM failed to see the dangers in the interconnectedness of international markets.**

"The very concept of safety through diversification–the basis of [LCTM's] own–security would merit rethinking."[2] According to Lowenstein, markets became closely linked. This made sense as the world grew closer thanks to technology and the elimination of many barriers (like the fall of the Berlin Wall and China's willingness to play ball in the global markets instead of remaining isolated). Other economies, like India's, only helped to make this more dangerous as all economies moved toward the same frequency.

2. **Leverage magnifies liquidity risk.**

The interconnectedness between world markets caused a lack of liquidity. According to Lowenstein, "'Liquidity' is a straw man. Whenever markets plunge, investors are [often] stunned to find that there are not enough buyers to go around. As [the famous economist John Maynard] Keynes observed, there [is no such thing as] 'liquidity' [of investment] for the community as a whole.[3] The mistake is in thinking that markets have a duty to stay liquid or that buyers will always be present to accommodate sellers . . . If you aren't in debt, you can't go broke and can't be made to sell, in which case 'liquidity' is irrelevant. But a leveraged firm may be *forced* to sell, lest fast-accumulating losses put it out of business. Leverage always gives rise to this same brutal dynamic, and its dangers cannot be stressed [enough]." In other words, excessive leverage is like playing with fire and eventually you will get burned. For the brief crisis in the markets spurred by the collapse of LTCM in 1998, the problem was people were ultimately forced to sell what they had (not necessarily what they should), which created a liquidity problem. That liquidity problem, in turn, affected the broader market. Effectively, your neighbor's problems became your own problems since leverage was involved.

Meanwhile, LTCM was relying on the concept of diversification, which is widely used in insurance and modern finance. By diversifying or spreading risk across many individual events (insurance) or different investments (finance), the potential for all of the events or investments to go against you is minimal to nearly nonexistent. Insurance counts on individual events when pricing risk (the law of averages with insurance risks truly diversified over many potential claims), whereas the modern financial concepts employed by LTCM were not as sophisticated, the intellectual firepower notwithstanding, and the company wrongly assumed that its diversification would protect it and a lack of liquidity would not be a problem. In fact, not only did they believe in their assumptions, but they also thought leverage would make their trades even more profitable.

From my experience as an option trader, the higher the probability of success, or a profit, on a trade, the lower the potential return. This should make sense from a probability or underwriting perspective. High-probability trades often require leverage to obtain the requisite profit since they usually have lower potential return. As a result, traders will sometimes leverage up that opportunity to get a meaningful profit. This is exactly what LTCM was doing—chasing what they thought were high-probability "nickels" in their quest for profits, using substantial leverage and therefore, risk, to move the needle.

As Lowenstein writes:

> [LTCM] preferred to reap a sure nickel than to gamble on making
> an uncertain dollar, because it could leverage its tiny margins like a
> high-volume grocer, sucking up nickel after nickel and multiplying

the process thousands of times. Of course, not even a nickel bet was *absolutely* sure. And as Steinhardt, the fund manager, had recently been reminded, the penalty for being wrong is infinitely greater when you are leveraged.[4]

It is for this reason and others that the investment approach I developed actively manages its option trades and does not depend on leverage.

With respect to LTCM, I don't believe the partners knew that their strategy was bound for disaster since most of their own capital was invested in the fund. It was a blind spot or miscalculation as opposed to willful recklessness. Their prior success and assurances from the portfolio managers led them to believe that temporary losses would eventually correct themselves and they should simply wait it out. They refused to believe they were at real risk and ignored the massive storm bearing down on them until it was too late. Not only did the storm end up wiping out their investments in the blink of an eye, but their massive use of leverage nearly brought down our entire financial system. As Keynes is often quoted, "Markets can remain irrational longer than you can remain solvent."[5]

### 3. Proper risk management is essential to long-term success.

There simply wasn't proper risk management at LTCM. This is not to say that the partners were not risk averse. In fact, their ideal trades were high-probability ones. However, no one was asking questions like what if this becomes a very crowded trade, what if the market stays irrational longer than we can stay solvent, what if we lose liquidity, or most important, what if we are forced to liquidate at an inopportune time due to our leverage?

Lowenstein explains: "Unlike at banks, where independent risk managers watch over traders, [LTCM] partners monitored themselves. Though this enabled them to sidestep the rigidities of a big organization, there was no one to call the partners [Larry Hilibrand and Victor Haghani] to account."[6]

Setting aside the obvious separation of duties that should be required in organizations like these, someone should have been tasked with oversight: poking holes, turning over every stone, and challenging the conventional wisdom.

What have we learned from this at Swan Global Investments? Numerous Swan team members are responsible for trade analysis and execution oversight. These individuals look at prospective and current trades from multiple angles and potential possibilities. Swan further encourages everyone to challenge management's positions. Healthy debate is essential to long-term success and is needed to invent, improve, and perfect. Worst-case scenarios not only have to be discussed, but also tested and planned for, so a firm can know what they will do and how they will do it when things don't go as expected.

Another erroneous assumption made by LTCM was that volatility was constant and that prices would trade in continuous time.[7] This would mean no gaps in prices, and as a result, there would be risk-free arbitrage because traders would have time to re-hedge and adjust their positions in real time. This, of course, is not even close to true in reality and shows how important it is to consider operational constraints of trading.

In addition to a lack of proper risk management, the book of trades managed by LTCM had too much complexity and too many trades. At some point, diversification alone, as it relates to market risk, does not work. You can't know with any certainty how the different trades are all going to work together. "And since many of its contracts were hedges that tended to cancel each other out, it was impossible to calculate [LTCM's] true economic exposure,"[8] writes Lowenstein.

### 4. The past is prologue.

This notion is dangerous in many areas of life, but especially when it comes to investments. The world is in a constant state of change ("delta" in option terminology), and the rate of change ("gamma" in option terminology) has increased dramatically due to the increase in knowledge and the integration of the global economy. The government has also increased this risk because investors often expect the government will somehow protect them from devastating market events. Traders often incorrectly assume the Federal Reserve will serve as a put option (or hedge) on the stock market, which ultimately causes problems when the market becomes overbought.

Once again, it should be noted that government cannot suspend the laws of nature. If government were the higher power, we would never have bear markets. As much as it might seem like it after a long bull market, bear markets have not been repealed but rather put off until later. Bear markets are a natural way of correcting markets, just like small forest fires make the likelihood of larger forest fires much smaller.

"In a strict sense, there wasn't any risk–if the world had behaved as it did in the past."[9] This quote by the economist and Nobel Laureate, Merton Miller, regarding LTCM's strategy, is astonishing in its falsehood. First, there is risk even if the "world had behaved as it did in the past." You might be able to define this risk and plan around it, but the risk is there. As some have said, risk can never be destroyed or completely removed, only transformed or shifted. Second, nothing (except for natural law) can be counted on as being constant. It is amazing that someone would use a false theory as the basis for managing risk. It is similar to using "always" or "never" statements.

As a basic rule, you always have to assume the worst or expect the unexpected. At Swan, we conduct stress tests on dozens of scenarios on a regular basis. We are constantly challenging our assumptions and comparing our strategy to competitors' and our expectations. Even without assuming the investment risk, you need to do this for business purposes.

Using variance around the mean, or standard deviation, as the definition of risk, as was widely used on Wall Street, was not enough. Major market crises or what the industry refers to as fat tail risks (the probability of an event or result three or more standard deviations away from the norm or standard distribution of results) are real and more frequent than people expect from a simple standard deviation model. It sounds good to say that your models will work within 2-3 standard deviations but 3-plus standard deviations must be considered in expected return calculations, especially when extreme leverage is used. The Brexit vote in the United Kingdom on June 23, 2016, provided a good reminder of this. The day after the vote, ten assets or major indices experienced moves of a 4 or greater standard deviation. The British pound experienced an astonishing 15 sigma event (sigma is a statistics terms that refers to the unlikelihood of events; the higher the number, the higher the unlikelihood). To put this in perspective, theoretically, this type of an event is only supposed to happen once every 1,090,000,000,000,000,000,000,000,000,000,000,000,000,000,000,000,000 years (1.09 quindecillion).

According to Lowenstein, "The conceit of modern Wall Street was that the closing prices printed in each day's [WSJ] were as reliable and predictive about the future as the actuarial tables of life insurance companies or the known and certain odds in shooting craps. And the conceit stemmed largely from [Robert] Merton and [Myron] Scholes."[10, 11]

We all know the probability of red or black in roulette. These probabilities are certainties over a large enough sample size. Conflating this simple calculation with probability calculations on complex markets is silly. We have less certainty with life insurance actuarial tables and even less certainty within the property and casualty industry. Markets would be at the bottom of this list.

Markets are simply real-time expressions of human sentiment, and human sentiment or human emotions can be unpredictable and highly irrational at times. Lowenstein notes in *Genius Failed*:

> There is a reason why financial markets run to extremes more often than coin flips–and more often than the "hundred-year storm" that [LTCM] partners would later cite as the culprit behind their disaster. A key condition of random events is that each new flip is *independent* of the previous one. The coin doesn't remember that it landed on tails three times in a row; the odds on the fourth flip are still fifty-fifty.
>
> But markets have memories. Sometimes a trend will continue just because traders expect (or fear) that it will.

Both investors and the LTCM partners believed "it would take a rare, 'calamitous' event–maybe a once-in-a-hundred-year flood–for [LTCM] to go seriously wrong. There would be times . . . when prices would deviate from the norm and when markets would move against [LTCM], costing it money. But for the markets in *all* of their trades to *consistently* depart from the norm would be a statistical freak, like rolling seven consecutive snake eyes or being hit by lightning twice."[12] Of course, in hindsight, we know this comparison to be factually wrong; the markets are more complex than dice and actuarial tables. The profit on betting on those types of risks is small because the risk is actually known.

It is important to note that this was not a hundred-year flood or a once-in-a-lifetime event, but rather something that happens regularly and probably more frequently as economies and markets become more tightly integrated.

Another flaw in LTCM's argument that excessive leverage is "safe" and in assuming that the improbable will never happen is this: If an event is going to happen at some point in the future, it really does not matter how much you make in gains prior to the event if those gains are all lost with leverage. In other words, you will lose 100 percent regardless of how much money you have already made if you keep going "all-in" with your "chips" and borrowed chips on the table. If you do not reinvest your profits or risk a small percentage of assets, then I could understand the gamble. It really comes down to properly managing and defining risk.

We frequently sit in rooms with smart and experienced people who tell us they can combine hundreds of strategies together and control the risk with precision. One thing I am nearly certain of is that you cannot control humans while investing. And while you may think you know your investment strategy, markets may change and the strategy may not adjust consistent with those changes. It goes back to my thesis about the problems or limitations with diversification: You cannot always count on diversification to work all the time. Unfortunately, the time you need it the most is when it probably works the least.

The interesting aspect from my perspective is that time and time again, financial engineering has been taken to its logical conclusion and failed. In the case of LTCM, conceptually, the strategy was initially correct, but not when "everyone" was doing it. With others jumping in creating a more crowded trade, the margin of error was small and the profits were small (nickels). Perhaps these academics tried to build a tower to the heavens by reading too much into their own press clippings, awards, or pats on the back received at cocktail parties.

**5. Crowded trades usually don't end well.**

A crowded trade is one in which a lot of people are doing the same thing and on the same side of the trade. This was one of the reasons for the collapse at LTCM. The firm was "feeding at the same trough" as many of its colleagues and peers. Everyone, over time, was ultimately doing the same type of bond arbitrage trades and could not get out when they needed to. An appropriate analogy is yelling fire in a crowded theater with limited exits. The partners underestimated their influence on the markets. As you will see in my analysis of *The Big Short*, most everyone was also doing the same trade, or making the same bets, prior to the 2008 Financial Crisis.

**6. Don't wander too far from your core competency.**

Success is often earned by taking the road less traveled, but in this case, LTCM's success was too much for its own good. Its assets grew beyond the capacity of its well-known trades, thus other traders or firms could see or anticipate its trades and front run or diminish their profitability. LTCM had to leave its core competency and begin trading in other areas outside its expertise. The firm might have been more successful over the long term if it had kept its assets small and stuck with what it knew.

**7. Go along to get along.**

There were countless examples of partners engaging in business with LTCM just to be part of the "in" crowd. Everyone was doing it, and no one was telling them not to. They participated regardless of whether they were going to profit from the relationship or the risk assumed. The level of collective fear of missing out was amazing to witness.

**8. Both the partners and investors got greedy.**

Why would you use that much leverage to get a return in the high teens after fees and expenses? Why not lever up a strategy that earns 8 percent with less probability of blowing up?

As an aside, just a few years after LTCM's infamous collapse, the original founder opened up another hedge fund called JWM Partners. It opened with around $250 million in assets under management and, by 2007, was managing more than $3 billion. Even after the disaster of LTCM, people were still entrusting their money to the same individuals who failed miserably before! As I've said, investors just don't learn from their mistakes. During the 2008 Financial Crisis, the main fund of JWM Partners lost 44 percent and the fund was closed in the summer of 2009. Shockingly, this individual opened a third hedge fund in 2010, running some of the same highly leveraged relative value arbitrage strategies that LTCM and JWM had used. That reminds me of an old saying: A fool and his money are soon parted.

In the end, when LTCM effectively blew up, many worried that it would create a domino effect and destabilize the financial system. So what did the government do? It bailed the firm out. The intention was to prevent a major fallout from happening, but all it did was send a very dangerous message: Take all the risk you want because you can get bailed out anyway. The pattern repeated in the dot.com bust a few years later, when the Fed lowered rates to stimulate the economy. This laid the groundwork for the housing crisis that arose eight years later.

## Reaping What You Sow—The Big Short

Unlike the LTCM crisis, which resulted from the arrogance of a limited few, the 2008 housing crisis came about mostly due to society at large, banks, and government leadership. As a result, the housing crisis had a much greater impact with far-reaching consequences—like nearly bringing down the world's economy.

The housing bubble inflated over decades due to a combination of bad policies and decisions by the government, lawmakers, regulators, ratings agencies, banks, homeowners, investors in homes, loan originators, realtors, appraisers, Wall Street firms, and ignorant investors. Any one of these participants could have stopped, or slowed, the problem from escalating to catastrophic levels by opting out of the game. Moral hazard was baked into the foundation of the subprime loans that get all the blame. But make no mistake, the rapid, significant rate decrease by the SGRs at the Federal Reserve, in an attempt to soften the landing from the dot.com bust, had unintended consequences and laid the foundation for the housing bubble. Natural law at work: Every action has a reaction.

Moral hazard plays a key role in all of this. Again, by definition, a moral hazard occurs when one party in a transaction has the opportunity to assume additional risks that negatively affect the other party.[13] More broadly, moral hazard is when the party with more information about its actions or intentions has a tendency or incentive to behave inappropriately from the perspective of the party with less information.

The originators of subprime loans[14] may have suspected that borrowers would not be able to maintain their payments in the long run, meaning the loans would not ultimately be worth much. The long-term viability of these loans wasn't a concern for these originators with so many buyers willing to take on that risk. Instead, they passed the risk to others; once an originator closed a loan, it was sold one or more times on the secondary market, often packaged together with other loans, until a firm that would service the loan bought the package. After selling the loans, the originators bore none of the risk and therefore had little or no incentive to care whether borrowers could repay their loans.

I don't hold any one politician or party responsible. I think the government collectively enacted a moral imperative to make it possible for everyone (or virtually everyone) in this country to own a home. A home of one's own became a proxy for the American Dream, and thus political rhetoric. In the wake of the dot.com bust, the growth of the nation's significant housing market, and all of the industries dependent on it (banks and lenders, insurers, homebuilders, carpenters, electricians, plumbers, real estate agents, manufacturers, land developers, and consumer spending spurred by accessing and spending the "equity" in one's home, to name a few), spurred US GDP and the economy at large. The government did everything it could to keep the mortgage party going, including imposing fines on banks that did not write a high enough quota of subprime loans, which existed to address the income inequality that prevented many from buying homes. While the intention was nice, the reality was not. The real-life outcome was the rise of subprime lenders who knowingly loaned money to people who could not pay it back. The government rarely considers the unintended consequences of its actions, and we all had to bear the consequences of that one. These policies let politicians feel good about themselves while Rome was burning.

Finance journalist Michael Lewis details the events that led up to the housing bubble and subsequent collapse in his great 2010 book-turned-movie, *The Big Short: Inside the Doomsday Machine*. At one point, Steve Eisman, a businessman known for shorting housing debt obligations, tells Lewis how these subprime companies would insist they were helping the consumer: "Because we're taking him out of his high interest rate credit card debt and putting him into lower interest rate mortgage debt. And I believed that story." Lewis writes that while these companies were happy to show off their earnings, what they "failed to disclose was the delinquency rate of the home loans they were making."[15] He goes on to explain how these companies took the loans and packaged them into mortgage bonds that they then sold to investors, effectively putting the risk on someone else.

"'What you want to watch are the lenders, not the borrowers,' [Eisman] said. 'The borrowers will always be willing to take a great deal for themselves. It's up to the lenders to show restraint, and when they lose it, watch out.' By 2003 he knew that the borrowers had already lost it."[16] Just so you know, both Eisman and Greg Lippmann, a hedge fund manager and key figure in Lewis's book, bet big on a housing market crash and made a killing.

Because the lenders sold many of the loans they made to other investors in the form of mortgage bonds, the industry was fraught with moral hazard. The original cast of subprime financiers had been sunk by the small fraction of the loans they made that they had kept on their books. After these initial subprime lenders realized the mistake of retaining some risk from loans they originated, newer incarnations endeavored to sell off all subprime loans. The market might have learned a simple lesson: Don't make loans to people who can't repay them. Instead it discovered another option: You can keep making these loans; just don't keep them on your books. Sell them off to the fixed-income departments of big Wall Street investment banks, which will in turn package them into bonds and sell them to investors.

As with LTCM, this was a crowded trade (mortgage-backed securities). There was a big punch bowl at the housing bubble party and plenty of guests. But many more who weren't involved still suffered a terrible hangover from it.

As the government was feeling good about its good intentions, for a myriad of reasons, regulators turned a blind eye. The real lesson here is that the Smartest Guys' good intentions often end with unintended consequences that gravely affect the common investor. The SGRs don't create every crisis, nor can they prevent every crisis, but when a serious problem arises (of their own making or not), they often compound the losses and make things worse by delaying the inevitable.

What does this mean for the investor? It means that we have to become more self-reliant to protect what we have worked so hard to accumulate and grow. The government creates policies that it thinks will help the many, but these policies often end up hurting the many and helping the few. The SGRs rarely consider the unintended consequences of their actions and often insulate themselves and their benefactors from those consequences. In this case, neither political party sounded the whistle loud enough to make a difference.

Government intervention intensifies market risk—the risk that is inherent in the very nature of investing and which cannot be diversified away. I have seen this connection in my own investing experience. By the time the 2008 Financial Crisis happened, I had already developed a solution that took into account market or systematic risk and was therefore less affected by the eventual crash. The Defined Risk Strategy did not directly short the mortgage market, but instead hedged against the stock market value, which ultimately reflected the pain of the crises, whatever the cause. The strategy I created and then built my firm around was designed to protect investors from what we believed could and would likely happen. The concept of a portfolio hedge is similar to having a life preserver as the *Titanic* sinks.

I go back to my earliest inspiration: Alan Greenspan's notion of irrational exuberance. What can you, as an investor, do when you disagree with the mainstream philosophy or approach? You design something that will protect you in that expected crisis while still covering your other bases. Hope for the best; prepare for the worst. Our strategy had to incorporate the fact that we could not know when a crisis would unfold but that we were confident one (or more) would occur at some point in time.

Here is a summary of lessons learned from the 2008 Financial Crisis and *The Big Short*:

1. Government's good intentions have unintended consequences. For example, the housing bubble looks a lot like the current student loan bubble.

2. Government cannot prevent every crisis, but it can in effect make a situation worse by delaying the inevitable; losses are compounded until eventually the crisis occurs.

3. People rely on government for protection that is not coming.

4. Government causes moral hazard.

5. People are not progressing; technology is.

6. Humans are self-centered, blame others, and will often take the path of least resistance.

7. The smartest minds are not infallible.

8. Cycles repeat because of human psychology and natural law.

9. Excessive leverage and debt are bad and will eventually have consequences. Natural law will eventually win out.

## The Fallout from the 2008 Financial Crisis—More Failure from Those We Trust

By now it should be quite clear that I have grave concerns about the political and economic headwinds the United States and the broader developed world are facing over the coming decades. Some people might regard politics and economics to be distant, esoteric topics with little impact on their day-to-day lives; however, there are real-world consequences to the decisions made (or not made) in Washington, D.C. For the purposes of this book, the most relevant are those that affect the financial markets and the investors who participate in them.

The 2008 Financial Crisis was certainly the biggest calamity to befall the markets since the Great Depression. The tools the world governments had at their disposal to address this were monetary, fiscal, and structural. While the response from these governments was massive, it was also off target and overdone in some areas.

The most obvious and most easily deployed tool for the SGRs was monetary policy. For the purposes of context, it is important to note that it is well known that Ben Bernanke, who served as chair of the Federal Reserve from February 2006 to February 2014, is an ardent student of the Great Depression. He falls into the school of thought that blames the majority of the damage wrought in the 1930s on a lack of liquidity and credit. With that backdrop, his subsequent actions should come as no surprise.

First, the Federal Reserve implemented the "Fed put," lowering interest rates in an attempt to encourage lending. This was coordinated with other central banks worldwide. What has been unique about this policy is the depth and duration of these rate cuts. Short-term interest rates have been near zero for almost a decade now and longer-term rates barely cover the cost of inflation. Only since 2017 have rates started to creep up.

Second, Congress began to take action with fiscal policy. A lot of ballyhoo was made about "shovel-ready" infrastructure projects that could be implemented immediately with a positive impact on local economies—just as soon as the government (i.e., taxpayer) taps were turned on and the money gushed out. The Economic Stimulus Act[17] in February 2008 and the American Recovery and Reinvestment Act (ARRA) in February 2009[18] authorized $152 billion and $787 billion of fiscal stimulus, respectively. The ARRA was later revised to $831 billion. Call me cynical, but I have yet to see a government project that turned out to be immediate or efficient.

In addition to federal government spending to stimulate the economy, Congress authorized the Treasury Department to make direct purchases of "troubled assets" to stem the panic sweeping through the markets in late 2008. The Troubled Asset Relief Program (TARP) was passed in October of that year to provide massive amounts of collateral to numerous systematically important financial institutions, regardless of whether those institutions actually needed the help.[19] TARP also bought up massive amounts of "toxic" assets. The idea was to stop markets from speculating on which domino would fall next.

Finally, and perhaps most controversially, there were several rounds of "open market operations," more commonly known as quantitative easing or QE. Trillions of dollars were created and injected into the financial system in an attempt to spur economic activity. During the dark days of 2008 and 2009, a much stronger case could be made for decisive government action to halt the panic. However, in the following years, the interventionist QE policies were just another government attempt to alter the fundamental supply and demand conditions that should drive the market. Many people believe QE, combined with this extended period of ultra-low interest rates, is sowing the seeds for the next financial crisis.

All of these unprecedented actions, especially those of the Federal Reserve, had an impact on markets, lowering rates and encouraging borrowing and risk-taking, resulting in the record buildup of debt securities on the Fed's balance sheet, as shown in Figure 3.1. It stands to reason that at some point there may be an unprecedented effect when all that debt on the Fed's balance sheet is unwound, or sold back to the markets. This is no secret. In 2012, then-Federal Reserve Open Market Committee (FOMC) board member (now the chair), Jerome "Jay" Powell, said, "Right now, we are buying the market, effectively, and private capital will begin to leave that activity and find something else to do. So when it is time for us to sell, or even to stop buying, the response could be quite strong; there is every reason to expect a strong response."[20]

─────────────── **Figure 3.1. Federal Reserve Bank Balance Sheet** ───────────────

■Securities Held Outright  ■ All Liquidity Facilities  ■ Support for Specific Institutions

*Source: St. Louis Federal Reserve*

It should be noted that prior to the 2008 Financial Crisis, QE was viewed as an experimental, unproven strategy. The only time it had been tried on a major scale was in Japan, whose economy has been in the doldrums since 1990. Massive monetary and fiscal expansion has not helped the Japanese resolve their core problems of deteriorating demographics and structurally rigid economies that don't allow for true competition, innovation, or entrepreneurial creative destruction. As the Japanese market over the last thirty years has illustrated, monetary and fiscal policy are easier to implement than structural changes, but ultimately much less effective. All the monetary tinkering by the Bank of Japan, even including a zero interest rate policy, had almost zero effect. Japan's economic growth rate from 1980 through 2017 averaged just about 0.5 percent per year.[21] Yet tragically, the response of most nations following the 2008 Financial Crisis was to replicate Japanese monetary and fiscal policies.

Increased central bank intervention, which can be seen most dramatically since the crash of 1987 in US stocks, has had a profound effect on the risk taking and debt accumulation around the globe, and in the United States in particular. In doing so, these "chief enablers" have inflated various asset class bubbles and exaggerated the historical equity and credit market cycles, creating larger reversions and nastier bear markets.

## Figure 3.2. Stock Market Valuation Based on S & P Companies' Book Values and Dividends

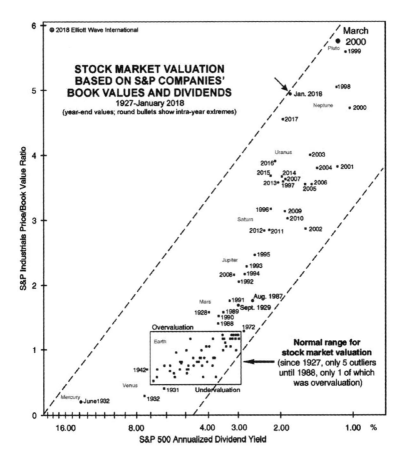

Source: *Elliot Wave Theorist; Barron's*

Figure 3.2, taken from the June 2018 issue of the *Elliot Wave Theorist*, is a unique, yet powerful visualization of this fact.[22] The chart shows the market valuation of S&P companies, based on their book values and dividends, from January 1927 through January 2018. The author overlays a solar system concept to plot the distances between planets to give the reader a reference for how far valuations of the market have gone on an annual basis.

The box labeled "normal range" indicates the valuations for the market that fell within that range, with only five exceptions, four of which deviated to the low side of the range. From the crash of 1987 and beyond, a period the author calls the Great Asset Mania begins. Every year, from 1988 through the start of 2018, the valuations exceed the previous normal range significantly, oftentimes deviating so far the author uses the distance from Earth to Pluto (in the case of 2000) as a reference. The arrow in the top right points to January 2018, where the valuations are "back to Neptune."

This is the work of the SGRs at their best. The graph shows the effect of central bank intervention and the SGRs' quest to stimulate aggregate demand—asset value inflation for US equities. This is simply math. Many might argue with the Elliot Wave Theory, or other theories, claims, or arguments put forth from Elliot Wave International, but it's hard to argue with the math in this chart. In addition, the last two bear markets, from 2000 to 2002 and from 2007 to 2009 with max drawdowns for the S&P 500 (peak to trough fall in the market price) of -47 percent and -55 percent, respectively, were more severe than all previous bear markets going back to the 1929 crash.[23]

The best way to help the economy and to normalize asset valuations is to rein in intervention and central management efforts by the SGRs, and instead let loose capitalism's animal spirits and let the "invisible hand" of noted eighteenth-century political economist Adam Smith guide individuals (and subsequently society) to their most advantageous activities. Yet the direction here in the United States is along a similar path of more central management and intervention. Gone are the days when most Americans would have agreed with President Ronald Reagan's saying, "The most terrifying words in the English language are 'I'm from the government, and I'm here to help.'" Look no further than President Barack Obama's first inauguration speech in 2009 or the widespread support of presidential candidate, Senator Bernie Sanders in 2016 if you want evidence that the majority of Americans now expect the government to have all the answers.

## Hope for the Best, Prepare for the Worst

Since no one on Earth can predict the outcome of our current fiscal quandary, logic demands an investment solution that doesn't rely on prediction and can profit in the widest range of market conditions. You need a strategy that can provide the greatest probability of success across the widest range of possible environments. An ideal strategy would also benefit from inevitable market cycles (i.e., both a bear and bull market). This comes down to having your assets on the highest branch in the tallest tree. These principles of an ideal strategy introduced in this book germinated and grew from a long-standing mindset and actions designed to accumulate wealth. These actions have included earning, saving, investing, and protecting money from all of the villains of wealth destruction (e.g., market cycles, inflation, taxes, confiscation).

As an investor, it is vital that you consider your desired outcome and view your investments in light of the circumstances outlined above. If the current situation cannot continue indefinitely, what path of wealth accumulation will take you to your desired outcome? Choose a strategy that will get you there whether the crisis appears, or the current bull market run lasts indefinitely.

Almost a hundred years ago, world champion chess player José Raúl Capablanca said, "In order to improve your game, you must study the endgame before everything else, for whereas the endings can be studied and mastered by themselves, the middle game and the opening must be studied in relation to the endgame."[24]

In light of today's low-dividend yield/low-interest rate environment, investors need to consider the likely endgame. If the current situation cannot continue indefinitely, how will bonds and stocks, or other asset classes, perform going forward?

We may not yet know how it will play out, or exactly when, but we do know that at some point natural law always wins, and the current bull market (another bubble in the making) ends in another painful market crisis. Those in power not only created these daunting problems but seem unwilling to fix them. Since there seems to be no end to the violation of natural law by the Smartest Guys in the Room, our only choice is self-reliance. We investors must take it upon ourselves to manage our individual wealth and future well-being. We can't wait for others to sweep in and save us, because they probably won't be able to. I believe investing in today's environment depends on hedging against many of the risks posed by our banking system and the powers that shape it.

# 4

# LIKELY OUTCOMES AND PASCAL'S WAGER

"The Fed has no endgame, and the chickens
are now coming home to roost."
—STANLEY DRUCKENMILLER,
DUQUESNE CAPITAL

Perhaps my assessment of the world economic situation and the perils investors face sounds alarmist to you. After all, it does run counter to what you've heard from the people you've always been taught to trust, those Smartest Guys in the Room (SGRs). Before I present you with further evidence to support my arguments for self-reliance in guarding your portfolio, I would like to offer a rhetorical framework that I believe will help you consider these questions with the seriousness they deserve. To better understand why investors should challenge the status quo and prepare themselves for the worst possible outcomes, let's take a moment to discuss Pascal's Wager.

## Pascal's Wager

This argument, introduced by the seventeenth-century French philosopher, mathematician, and physicist Blaise Pascal, is perhaps the most critical concept you should take away from this book and apply in your investing lives. Pascal posits in what is essentially an argument in apologetic philosophy[1] that humans bet with their lives that either God exists or does not exist. Based on a lifelong series of notes, his theory was published posthumously as the book *Pensées* ("Thoughts") in 1678. Historically, Pascal's Wager charted new territory in probability theory, marked the first formal use of decision theory, and anticipated future philosophies such as existentialism, pragmatism, and voluntarism.[2]

Pascal proposed that the stakes are infinite if God exists. So, *if* there is even a small probability that there is a God, then a rational person should seek to embrace that belief and live life accordingly. If God does not exist, an individual believing in God will have a finite loss (forgoing some pleasures, luxury, etc.). If, however, God does exist, then believers stand to receive infinite gains (as represented by eternity in Heaven) and avoid infinite losses (eternity in Hell).[3]

How does this relate to the global economy and investors?

In the pages that follow, I am going to lay out three possible outcomes we may face if the government and economy continue on their path. In the end, we can approach the situation in two ways: The economy will either face a major crisis or collapse that affects us gravely, or it won't. Like Pascal's believer, investors who live in acceptance of a possible collapse will not lose much if it never manifests. However, just as not believing in God could result in infinite loss if it turns out that God does exist, denying the possibility of an economic collapse could also lead to infinite loss if that collapse occurs and one is unprepared.

## Wagering on the Best Worst-Case Scenario

Let's take a moment to look at some critical numbers surrounding growth and current Federal Reserve policies. Hedge fund legend Stanley Druckenmiller has said of the Fed that

> They stumble from one short-term fiscal or monetary stimulus to the next despite overwhelming evidence that they only produce a sugar high and grow unproductive debt that impedes long-term growth. Moreover, the continued decline of global growth despite unprecedented stimulus the past decade suggests we have borrowed so much from our future and for so long that the chickens are now coming home to roost.[4]

He goes on to warn us:

> This is a big, big gamble to be manipulating the most important price in free markets, interest rates. These [bond] purchases are canceling market signals. The bond market and the stock market have provided wonderful signals for many years as to potential problems. And when you cancel those signals . . . you could run into a problem . . . I don't know when it's going to end, but my guess is it's going to end very badly.[5]

This is not some obscure doomsday prediction by a fringe radical, but a thoughtful diagnosis of what is happening from someone who puts his money where his mouth is.

The World Bank forecast GDP growth of lower than 2 percent for advanced economies through at least 2018. In April 2016, the International Monetary Fund (IMF) titled its periodic *World Economic Outlook* report, "Too Slow for Too Long." In it, the IMF lowered its best- and worst-case scenarios for world growth.

## Figure 4.1. Risks to the Global Outlook

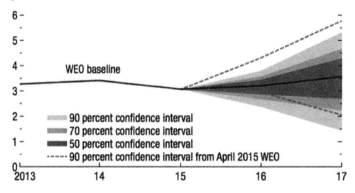

With a lower baseline forecast for global growth and a slightly wider confidence band around the baseline forecast, the fan chart shows that risks of weaker growth outcomes have increased.

*Source: IMF*

The Fed forecasts US growth even lower for the long run.

──────────────── **Figure 4.2. Change in Real GDP** ────────────────

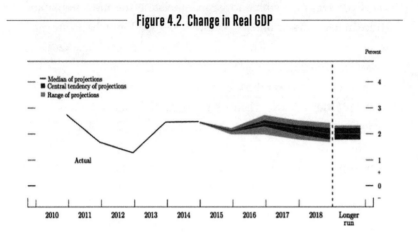

*Source: Federal Reserve*

Most politicians do not seem disturbed by these projections. In fact, they act as if raising or lowering federal tax rates by 5 percent or less (as has happened since 1992) determines whether or not birds fly south for the winter. In other words, they think a tax rate change will make everything OK in the world. Most politicians and Federal Reserve officials have been making similar declarations about deficits and debt for decades, as if talk will inoculate them from the inevitable day of reckoning. They have failed to take any decisive action.

Nevertheless, a correction is coming. I'm not necessarily saying we will experience a crash that "ends life as we know it," although an argument exists for a scenario involving massive social upheaval on a global scale. More likely, the assertion of natural law will cause quite a bit of pain and suffering to those who can least afford it. Worse, the correction will likely be much larger than it would have been if those in power had let smaller natural fires occur. Now, it appears nature will require a super fire to clear out the dead brush.

The extent of correction will likely fall somewhere between what Japan has experienced since the late 1980s and a more massive collapse (e.g.,

2007–09) that significantly diminishes most investors' net worth. A 50 percent to 70 percent collapse in global prices is not that unrealistic, especially since we have had two 50-plus percent sell-offs since 2000 (not to mention Japan's -80 percent stock market drawdown from 1989 to 2009).

There are many possible outcomes, and almost all of them are negative for today's investors. Most expert projections align to a degree that one can say confidently that traditional expected returns for the assets of a typical, diversified portfolio will fall well short of what investors may expect and most likely need to reach their long-term financial objectives. See the table titled "What the Experts Say" in Chapter 5 (Figure 5.6) for a review of expert return forecasts for stocks and bonds over the next five to ten years.

However, the financial industry at large would have investors believe otherwise. Why else would they continue advocating for the same portfolio constructions and investing approaches for decades? Applying Pascal's theory, we can examine the situation in two ways: There will be a massive economic correction that can irreparably damage the remainder of investors' lives or there won't. Since the industry hasn't seriously changed its ways since the last bear market, many believe the latter.

The world doesn't currently face a 50/50 proposition between infinite financial success and utter financial destruction. Rather, smaller probabilities exist for hundreds of possibilities. While we cannot expect to predict exactly how things may transpire, we can venture an educated guess on the three most likely outcomes and weigh the probability of each one. For simplicity's sake, we are going to attach a one-third probability to each.

## Swan's View of Likely Outcomes

### Option 1: Good Outcome

In our Good Outcome scenario, most investors' portfolios do not sustain significant losses, but they are unlikely to gain much either. Thus, the best case is really only *somewhat* positive.

The investor achieves below average returns until these economic problems are resolved, perhaps for the next twenty to thirty years or more. Crestmont Research, an independent researcher of financial markets, made a strong case in a market research report for why today's investors *cannot* enjoy a repeat of the long-term historic average annual return of US large-cap equities (approximately 10 percent per year): The best case for equities going forward is probably in the 2 percent to 4 percent range, up to 5 percent if generous.[6] At Swan, we predict that fixed income also has a zero percent chance of returning to its historic long-term average of between 5 percent and 6 percent and will, at best, deliver a maximum of 2 percent to 3 percent.

Given these arguments, in our Good Outcome scenario, the best annual return forecast for a typical diversified portfolio (60 percent stocks, 40 percent bonds) is probably 3 percent.

Under these conditions, very few people will reach their financial goals (comfortable retirement) simply because most do not have any real net worth or savings. At the end of 2015, a survey by Google Consumer Surveys for Bankrate showed that approximately 62 percent of American adults have less than $1,000 in savings. Another recent study says that 78 percent of full-time workers live paycheck to paycheck.[7] To reach their goals, most investors need to grow their retirement nest egg using investment returns (in risk assets or real estate) or receive a healthy inheritance.

Worse, when you account for the many severely underfunded pension plans, which have little or no chance of achieving successful returns, many pensioners will likely receive a painful surprise of much lower income than expected.

This Good Outcome also does not take inflation into account. While the government would have everyone believe inflation is only 2 percent, I have a difficult time finding anyone who actually believes this number. Adjusting for actual inflation, the real return in this "good" scenario is probably 0 percent to 2 percent. For example, an investor saving $15,000 per year for thirty years and continually investing at 1 percent real growth would end up with $450,000 in savings and have just shy of $100,000 in investment return growth, before any taxes. This assumes no major bear markets that significantly reduce that account balance around the time the investor wants to retire. This is what the Good Outcome looks like.

## Figure 4.3. How Much Money Americans Have in Savings, 2014-2018

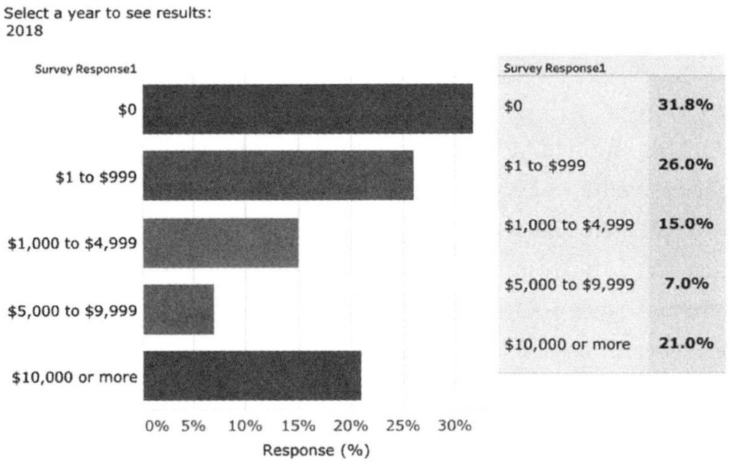

Select a year to see results:
2018

| Survey Response1 | | |
| --- | --- | --- |
| $0 | | 31.8% |
| $1 to $999 | | 26.0% |
| $1,000 to $4,999 | | 15.0% |
| $5,000 to $9,999 | | 7.0% |
| $10,000 or more | | 21.0% |

| Survey Response1 | 2014 | 2015 | 2016 | 2017 | 2018 |
| --- | --- | --- | --- | --- | --- |
| $0 | 44.5% | 28.0% | 34.0% | 39.0% | 31.8% |
| $1 to $999 | 28.5% | 13.0% | 35.0% | 18.0% | 26.0% |
| $1,000 to $4,999 | 8.9% | 10.0% | 11.0% | 11.0% | 15.0% |
| $5,000 to $9,999 | 4.2% | 5.0% | 4.0% | 4.0% | 7.0% |
| $10,000 or more | 13.8% | 14.0% | 15.0% | 25.0% | 21.0% |

Source: GOBankingRates.com

While truly rich people can survive making a 2 percent to 3 percent return per year, even if there is no real increase in purchasing power, the middle and upper-middle class face a substantial decline in their standard of living. Those at the bottom of the economic food chain will struggle more than they do now and will likely lose a lot of services that they currently enjoy as state and local governments are forced to cut back.

## Option 2: Average Outcome

In our Average Outcome, people take the pain in the form of inflation to avoid the unappealing prospect of an all-out collapse in the financial system. In the name of preventing destruction and social upheaval, the government comes up with some questionable attempt to spread the damage over the next twenty to thirty years. This may take the form of monetization of our debt or some other elaborate scheme involving the confiscation of accounts and forcing the population to buy government debt in the name of the common good. Consider US Treasury policy during the Great Depression. On April 5, 1933, President Franklin D. Roosevelt signed Executive Order 6102 "forbidding the hoarding of gold coin, gold bullion, and gold certificates within the continental United States." This means that American citizens were forced to surrender their gold to the US Treasury or face prosecution.[8] Private individuals were prohibited from owning more than a very small amount of gold for more than forty years—until 1974. Such government actions could happen again.

This outcome, although not the worst, still comes at an ugly loss of personal freedoms—financial and social—as people are forced to subsidize waste, fraud, and abuse. We end up paying for the sins of our forebears, robbing future consumption to pay for past consumption.

In the Average Outcome, 5 percent inflation would likely last longer than any of our individual lifetimes. Everyone would be forced to swallow this bitter pill as the only way out. At best, it would mean no real return from investments in most years and probably a loss in purchasing power. And, after twenty to thirty years, some uglier crisis would still be likely. Sustaining an increase in inflation for a prolonged period kills the sense of progress for most of the population as they see no way for themselves or their children to move up the socioeconomic ladder—they're trapped.

Quite frankly, this situation is already playing out for those not fortunate enough to have previously secured financial or real assets. Pew Research conducted a study in 2017 that shows that the majority of Americans, as well as the populace of many other developed nations, are pessimistic about their children's future.[9] The lower-middle and middle classes have experienced this pain for the past few decades.

I don't see a lot of risk taking in such an environment. Likely, before a government seizure or monetization of the average person's assets, the wealth of the truly rich would already have been taken, hidden, or consumed, leaving them far less likely to take financial risks. Oppression kills incentive and without incentive you have no growth.

Perhaps some entrepreneurs living in the Average Outcome scenario will do something out of a sense of moral obligation or to accrue political power. Given the dismal historic examples of entrepreneurship under socialism and communism, this seems like a long shot.

I believe the SGRs are aiming for the Average Outcome—the one that seems most logical to them. The politicians blame the rich—the 1 percent and above. The rich, academics, and economists blame the politicians. Average people believe whoever makes them feel better and blame those who don't. Much of this is already playing out—just tune into the nightly news.

The Average Outcome scenario does not sound fun.

### Option 3: Bad Outcome

The Bad Outcome, or worst-case scenario, takes a heavy toll on society, beginning with a devastating economic crisis or collapse, resulting in the widespread selling of assets. I believe such an event is likely to be credit-driven, given the sheer size of global indebtedness, both at public and private levels. As the economy inevitably contracts, debt problems are exacerbated as there is less money flowing into the hands of debtors. Interest rates will rise and credit will significantly tighten, if not halt altogether, as those who lent money and were left unpaid refuse to lend again. Most investors' portfolios will be permanently damaged. Investors will likely sell all of their non-cash financial assets at or near the bottom (in normal psychology, we sell out of fear and buy out of greed) and never invest again. I would expect 60 percent to 90 percent losses almost across the board.

The math behind investment returns proves that it is very difficult to recover from a 90 percent loss. The more you lose, the more it takes to recover and break even.

## Figure 4.4. The Math Behind Investment Returns

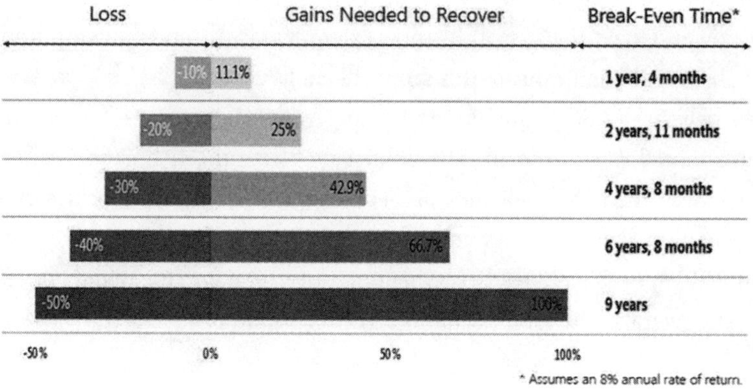

| Loss | Gains Needed to Recover | Break-Even Time* |
|------|------------------------|------------------|
| -10% | 11.1% | 1 year, 4 months |
| -20% | 25% | 2 years, 11 months |
| -30% | 42.9% | 4 years, 8 months |
| -40% | 66.7% | 6 years, 8 months |
| -50% | 100% | 9 years |

| -50% | 0% | 50% | 100% |

* Assumes an 8% annual rate of return.

*Source: Swan Global Investments*

Losing 10 percent will only require 11 percent to break even. That doesn't seem so bad, until you look a little farther down the line. Losing 40 percent to 50 percent requires 67 percent to 100 percent to recover. Making 100 percent takes a very long time, period. With the state of the economy, good luck getting near that. The odds of those returns are very, very slim.

I'm not alone in recognizing that such a Bad Outcome is in the range of possibilities. The SGRs are making moves to either stave off revolutionary calls from the suffering, fed-up masses, or to remain largely insulated from potential civil unrest and backlash. We're seeing a new trend of tech titans creating underground bunkers in New Zealand or elsewhere.[10] Others are transferring their wealth into shelters like hard assets, cryptocurrencies, or even gaming currencies. They realize the debt levels are too vast, the wage gap is expanding, and the opportunity, if not the promise, of prosperity is not being realized by larger segments of the nation. They know the bowl of spiked punch runs out eventually.

The Bad Outcome involves massive confiscation or forced widespread "sharing" of the pain. Bond investors (creditors) will suffer significant, if not total, losses as public debt is restructured, and many debts go unpaid. We only need to look around to see how this could play out. In July 2018,

Senators Elizabeth Warren and Bernie Sanders and four other senators introduced a bill to restructure Puerto Rico's $73 billion in public debt.[11] Their plan is essentially to write off the majority of that debt, using roughly $15 billion of fresh taxpayer funds to pay selected creditors. Those deemed less fortunate, in this case certain Puerto Rican pensioners and businesses, for example, would receive a payment in some lesser amount than they were owed. Meanwhile other creditors deemed unworthy of protection, like bond insurers, large financial firms, hedge fund investors (or as Senator Warren referred to them as, "vultures"), would be forced to take their losses in full. Here the politicians (some of the worst SGRs) assume the role of trustee and pick winners and losers based on political expediency. As an added bonus, the bill provides territories like Puerto Rico the ability to reset their debt once every seven years. Regardless of whether this bill passes, it may serve as a blueprint for how municipalities, states, and nations "reset" the larger scale debts they simply cannot repay.

The calls for a guaranteed income, more recently championed by the super-rich Silicon Valley elite, may belie a larger realization by the SGRs and their richest benefactors that the bottom half of the population, who are counting on retirement income from pensions and various municipal and federal bonds, may not get all they were promised.[12] A guaranteed income could at some level replace the interest income assumed by these investors and ameliorate the fact that their bond investments may be worth much less (or worthless) at some point.

In the Bad Outcome, the short term will be miserable. Yet, ironically, it might provide opportunity for future generations to get on better footing. It pulls the Band-Aid off quickly, and then allows the healing process to begin. However, that healing process may take many years, even decades, while the event and subsequent collapse would cause permanent financial damage for generations of people. In this scenario, healing would begin only after a period of widespread financial pain that typically follows a massive economic fallout: civil unrest, revolution, or war.

The Bad Outcome may only be possible if the SGRs and current power players lose control of the situation. Make no mistake; they are willing to die on the hill to avoid this outcome. The asset class bubbles witnessed over the past several decades are the result of attempts to control economies and pursue aggregate demand to any end in order to avoid serious periods of deflation, i.e., another Great Depression. In my humble opinion, nature and natural law, by definition, are bigger, stronger, and more powerful than the human powers in control.

What does this mean for our clients, or other investors who want to grow and protect capital?

I would only invest in equities—don't invest in bonds, or at least not public bonds or bonds issued by highly leveraged corporations. In the short to mid-term, low rates hurt savers and any rise in rates will reduce bond values. In the long term, municipal and government treasuries will take big cuts, if not be totally written off. To the extent that the crises inherent in the Bad Outcome bleed into the equity market, investors can at least use the means of hedging to protect those asset values. By avoiding bonds as an asset class, those investors in hedged equity are on the highest branch in the tallest tree. If you're questioning whether such debt write-offs or restructurings occur, well, that brings us back to Pascal's Wager. Even if there is a small chance of such an outcome, will you wager your financial future on it? In my opinion, the best wager to make for your stored value (wealth) in any of these scenarios is investing in hedged equity and avoiding bonds.

All three outcomes offer dire circumstances for investors. No matter which you believe the most likely, or if you believe a correction will come at all, the stakes are high. Only by looking at all possible outcomes can we properly determine appropriate preparation. As with Pascal's Wager, I believe it's better to acknowledge the very real possibility of the worst outcome, however small the perceived chance, rather than ignore it and have it come about. It's better to be prepared for the worst in case it does happen.

Let's look at some corollaries between the logic of Pascal's Wager (excerpts from *Pensées*, part III, section 233) and our assessment of the likely outcomes, which we will call "Swan Corollaries":

1. Pascal's Idea: God is or God is not. Reason cannot decide between the two alternatives.

*Swan Corollary*: The global economy is going to collapse or it is not. You don't know which is going to happen. Reason and data can't completely predict the outcome.

2. Pascal's Idea: A game is being played where heads or tails will turn up.

   *Swan Corollary*: An endgame will occur whether or not you believe it to be so. There are two simple outcomes—one where everything will be manageable and one where everything will not. The basis for the two outcomes is already being played out now.

3. Pascal's Idea: You must wager. It is not optional.

   *Swan Corollary*: You are making a bet whether you know you are or not. If you stick with the traditional diversified portfolio Wall Street and the industry have used for decades, then you have placed your bet. As with the non-believer, you can expect a painful time of it if the correction comes. Like Pascal's believer, the proactive option involves finding a better way to invest and prepare.

4. Pascal's Idea: Let us weigh the gain and the loss in wagering that God is. Let us estimate these two chances. If you gain, you gain all; if you lose, you lose nothing.

   *Swan Corollary*: Let us weigh the potential gains and losses in wagering that the economy will have a catastrophic crisis or collapse and estimate these two chances. If you protect yourself, you gain your financial life or you lose very little.

5. Pascal's Idea: Wager, then, without hesitation that God is. There is here an infinity of an infinitely happy life to gain, a chance of gain against a finite number of chances of loss, and what you stake is finite. And so, our proposition is of infinite force, when there is the

finite to stake in a game where there are equal risks of gain and of loss, and the infinite to gain.

*Swan Corollary*: Change your financial outlook on the assumption that a bad endgame is going to happen. You should be rewarded by better preserving your financial life.

6. Pascal's Idea: But some cannot believe. They should then "at least learn your inability to believe" and "endeavor then to convince" themselves.

*Swan Corollary*: As a result of the analysis, logically there is only one real choice. If you can't accept this, then try to convince yourself of it because the cost of failing to believe is enormous and the cost of believing is minimal.

As we cannot determine how this is going to end, we are all forced to gamble. I ask readers to analyze the current fiscal and monetary situation, demographics, and state of humankind from an individual personal responsibility perspective: Are you prepared for a potential bad outcome?

## Analysis with Decision Theory

Like Pascal's Wager regarding the existence of God, most of us are playing a game with our financial lives regardless of whether we recognize it or not. In Pascal's assessment, participation in this wager is not optional. Merely by existing in a state of uncertainty, we are forced to make a choice between the available courses of action.

Estimates of our Good, Average, and Bad Outcomes follow in Figure 4.5. For simplicity's sake, we will assume that each of these outcomes has the same probability of occurring. The values in this matrix are assumed to be annualized ten-year targets. Expected returns are calculated according to the values and probability of occurrence.

## Figure 4.5.

|  | Real Likely Return | Nominal Likely Return | Probability of Occurrence |
| --- | --- | --- | --- |
| Good Outcome | 0 to -2% | 2-4% | 33% |
| Average Outcome | -3 to -5% | 0% | 33% |
| Bad Outcome | -7 to -13% | -10-13% | 33% |
| Exp Return | -5.00% | -2.83% |  |
| 10 yr. Target | Annualized return expectations for various scenarios | | |
| Good = | Current situation, muddled growth, nothing much happens | | |
| Average = | Inflate our way out of the mess | | |
| Bad = | -50 percent to -75 percent losses over 10 years* | | |

* Note: Hypothetical assumptions. Real return is after inflation.

Assuming equal probability for each outcome, expected returns over the next ten years range from -2.83 percent to -5.00 percent—a bleak outlook in direct contrast to our government's predictions for our future.

Study the endgame, as the Cuban chess master José Raúl Capablanca advised. Even if you ignore the mathematical calculation of expected returns, the potential loss for the worst-case scenario is so big that you have to account for it even if you assume a small probability. As with Pascal's Wager, the cost for being wrong about unbelief far outweighs being wrong about the other possibilities. If there is even a small possibility that things will not end well, a rational person would argue that you need to take that small possibility into account when planning your investment life. We must hope for the best but prepare for the worst. Considerations of risk and return are paramount. History and past solutions won't tell you everything you need to know about the current investment environment nor help you play out the endgame unscathed.

I suspect the Bad Outcome has the highest probability of eventually coming to pass, especially in light of the Federal Reserve's decision to sacrifice fixed-income investors and savers for the "greater good." Would they have taken such drastic measures to avoid the inevitable unless they thought the probability was greater than 50 percent? Their actions speak loudly of their fear of the Bad Outcome and indicate that they believe this to be a real possibility, not some Chicken Little cry by doomsayers.

## Technology—an Endgame Wild Card

Is there no way out? Well, there is at least a wild card at play here that I feel should be addressed—technology.

Improvements from technology could potentially offset some—but not all—of the negative effects of excessive debt, perhaps lengthen periods of expansion (bull markets), and create more wealth for some. Some even claim the ongoing technological revolution—automation, digitalization, artificial intelligence—will be as impactful as the Industrial Revolution. What do we mean by improvements? Will it be enough to change the economy forever, as some have postulated? Automation and artificial intelligence could have a positive effect on productivity in many areas of the economy, potentially lowering the cost of many goods and services. In addition, scientific breakthroughs in medical technology and biochemical areas could benefit society. I don't believe these can completely offset what is coming; rather, they have the potential to mitigate some of the effects.

A recent study by McKinsey and Company titled, "A Future That Works: Automation, Employment, and Productivity," claims that the majority of occupations (60 percent) can expect about 30 percent of their tasks to be automated; 5 percent can be completely automated. Functions that may be replaced by robots include the following:[13]

- Food and hospitality, 74 percent
- Transportation and warehousing, 61 percent
- Manufacturing, 54 percent
- Retail, 53 percent

Some argue that the coming technological revolution will be every bit as disruptive as the shift from agrarian to industrial production. The upside is expected productivity growth on a global basis by 0.8 percent to 1.4 percent annually. But that comes with a host of changes that may offset the "benefits" derived from technology. For instance, how much of these productivity gains will be offset by falling employment and the costs of excessive borrowing over the last thirty years on a global level? If productivity gains mean lower production costs, will companies in the developed world continue to export labor to developing nations? How much will that transform the social and economic advancements in those nations, which have benefited from the exportation of labor from developed nations?

Many forward-looking writers and thinkers, who care more about the future than next quarter's earnings report, have been debating these issues:

- Are gains from technology being concentrated in the hands of a few monopolistic or oligarchic organizations?
- Will all gains from productivity flow solely to the income statements of these few companies?
- Where does that leave the mass of workers who will be rendered redundant by technology?
- Will the "losers" from technological arms races demand more from the state or world order?
- Will the state be in a position to meet those demands?

There are many, like the tech titans and thought leaders, who believe that these developments will render my Good/Average/Bad Outcomes irrelevant. They argue that the automation and digitalization of industries will usher in a utopian-like era of reduced costs, reduced workloads, more leisure, and less stress. This idea is not new. In 1930, noted economist John Maynard Keynes asserted that his grandchildren would work a fifteen-hour week.[14] His theory began with the well-grounded concept that technology would increase productivity, but then he made some unrealistic assumptions about human nature in asserting that the developments would increase workers' free time and make their work hours more valuable. But that is not what we've been seeing the last couple of decades, at least not for all segments of the labor market. This next chart shows that lower-income workers are at risk of more dislocation or replacement by automation. These workers must either quickly adapt to acquire new, desirable skills, or be forced to seek assistance, thus creating more social cost-burden on the economy.

— **Figure 4.6. Automation May Create Worse Outcomes for Lower-Income Workers** —

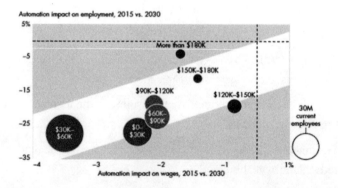

*Source: US Bureau of Economic Analysis; US Bureau of Labor Statistics; Bain Macro Trends Group analysis, 2017.*

Meanwhile, the owners of the means of production and the top tranches of management and in-demand skilled labor will enjoy an ever-growing share of the compensation or benefits from technology.

## Figure 4.7. Labor's Share of GDP Is Already Declining; Increased Automation May Accelerate This Trend

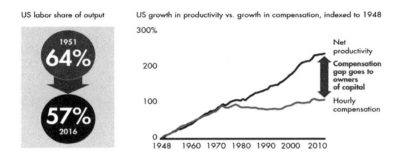

*Sources: US Bureau of Labor Statistics; Economic Policy Institute; Bain Macro Trends Group analysis, 2017.*

*Notes: US labor share of output is five-year moving average; labor share is for nonfarm sectors; data is for average hourly compensation of production/nonsupervisory workers in private sector and net productivity of total economy; net productivity is growth of output of goods and services minus depreciation per hour worked.*

Investors who believe they will fall into this group should keep in mind the timeline for this disruption to occur. Technology advances quickly but society takes time to adopt and implement technologies, especially those that replace 30 percent of an entire industry's workforce. So investors reading this and other materials on the age of the robots and how they will change everything need to remember that even the experts are talking about a time span of about thirty years to more than eighty from 2016.[15] That's a lot of market cycles between then and now, by the way, for you to have to save, invest, and achieve long-term goals in the face of the more pressing issues I've covered thus far.

In the end, I predict that technological disruption will actually increase the chances of the Average or Bad Outcome. The real losers will be our once-protean middle class. Unlike the owners of corporations in the past, the tech titans of Silicon Valley are becoming modern-day oligarchs who seem to have no interest in their workers becoming homeowners or moving up the class ladder. "Their agenda seems to include forever-denser, super-expensive rental housing for their primarily young, and often short-term, employees . . . All the middle and upwardly aspiring working class gets is the right to pay ever more taxes, while they watch many of their children devolve into serfs, dependent on alms and subsidies for their survival," wrote urban studies expert Joel Kotkin in the *Orange County Register*.[16]

What could this end up looking like? It is too early to tell but numerous studies have highlighted the potential of increasing productivity and greater concentration of capital. One study has projected that the top 0.1 percent will have about as much wealth as the entire middle class by 2050, as these factors begin to widen the spread further between the oligarchy and the "labor" population.

## Potential Problems from This Trend

Technology is a wild card, yes, but it has never indelibly changed human nature and therefore will not permanently change the economy or the nature of markets. Natural law will prevail. As long as humans decide when to buy and sell investments, markets will reflect their emotions and nature. I believe technology will affect the trajectory but not substantially alter our course from the three likeliest outcomes discussed above. So investors should begin with the endgame in mind.

- How is the debt going to be paid off or restructured? Who is going to suffer the most?
- How can 30 percent to 40 percent of the population pay for 100 percent of the population?
- Where does demand come from?

- Will the 30 percent to 40 percent have a profit motive or will it be based on altruism or survival (i.e., avoid the proverbial pitchforks)?

- What are the psychological effects of having 60 percent to 70 percent of people around the globe unproductive?

- What will be the impact on the stock markets and among technology companies and other affected corporations?

The technological transformation that will occur in the next few decades will most assuredly have a profound impact on the economy around the globe. Labor markets, national economics, and most industries will be dramatically changed. Of course, the temporary imbalances caused by this seismic shift will eventually be resolved, and new opportunities and risks will arise for both the labor force and the markets. There will be winners (and some very big winners), and there will be losers (and some very big losers), both from a company and an individual perspective. So investors looking to technology will likely have just as much difficulty as ever in picking and timing those opportunities and risks. As nineteenth-century polymath and philosopher Oliver Wendell Holmes, Sr. once said, "Prophesy as much as you want but always hedge."

At Swan, we don't believe that the SGRs, or technology, can change the laws of nature and prevent the inevitable. We do, however, believe that their actions have both postponed the day of reckoning and made the inevitable much worse in the process. By snuffing out the small fires that naturally clear out the brush, they have insulated us from tolerable pain and set us up for a storm of immense magnitude causing intolerable pain.

Are you really willing to risk your financial well-being? Do you really have that much faith in humankind's Smartest Guys to overcome the laws of nature?

Remember, you lose little to nothing if you plan for the worst and no collapse materializes—a few pleasures and luxuries. If you take heed and properly plan according to Swan's view of likely outcomes, you will have space reserved on the ark, so to speak. The cost of preparing for something that does not occur for many years, or not at all, is nothing compared to trying to weather the storm after a lack of preparation. Regardless of your faith or hope in the Smartest Guys, preparation is the only sound choice. Of course, it's mentally easier to go along with their master plan, placing your hope in progress and people's perfectibility.

However, if you believe our problems cannot be resolved without significant pain, you must pursue every option that protects against the inevitable. People incorrectly think they don't have any choices. This book exists to let you know you do have choices outside the traditional mainstream groupthink.

We believe that successful navigation of our current, problematic circumstances starts with confronting reality and follows through by adopting a solution that encompasses all possibilities. People often accept poor choices because they don't know there is a better way. There is.

First, let me show you the precise flaws with the traditional way of investing.

## 5

# LIMITATIONS OF MODERN PORTFOLIO THEORY AND TRADITIONAL INVESTING STRATEGIES

I started working at fourteen. Throughout my teens I worked a lot, and I worked hard: I launched my own landscaping and maintenance business, cleaned my dad's office, and worked as a stagehand. By the time I graduated high school, I had saved $11,000.

I used most of the money I made from landscaping plus Christmas and birthday gifts to start investing. It was investing, as opposed to trading, because I had longer-term goals and I wasn't interested in short-term speculation. I began by spreading out my savings into stocks and bonds via mutual funds, as well as in gold and silver coins. As I began that journey in 1981, I had no idea it was near the start of one of the biggest bull markets in history (both for stocks and bonds).

My passion for investing intensified in college. From ages twenty to twenty-eight, I spent a considerable amount of time learning various investment philosophies and strategies. I read dozens of books and attended workshops, even real estate and tax lien seminars. I was searching for the best solution—the holy grail of investing—and kept coming up short. I tried to accelerate the learning process and stress-tested everything with actual capital.

I began with the usual portfolio constructions pushed by the industry and most investment guides at that time (and today, for that matter):

allocating to various assets for diversification and to get the best risk/return trade-off. But during the '87 crash, the '90 recession, and the bear market that followed, I lost more than 20 percent of my money. I was doing the right things according to traditional wisdom: investing in a diversified portfolio of stocks, bonds, and cash and not putting all my eggs in one basket. If the promise of asset allocation and diversification was to minimize or offset some losses, it clearly wasn't working the way the Smart Guys theorized. During those early investing experiences, I began to see flaws in these supposedly "diversified portfolios."

Trading, timing, and stock-picking strategies required exhaustive research and felt like constant churning just to break even (if I was lucky). I also realized that paying others to tell me what they thought was going to happen meant little unless they were putting their money where their mouth was (i.e., investing beside me). If the authors of a financial newsletter did not actually put significant portions of their own money in their recommendations or strategies, I wasn't interested. Even then, they could still end up being very wrong. Still, if I was going to invest based on someone else's advice, they had to be eating their own cooking, if you will.

My personal experiences gave me insight into what investors should want in a strategy and helped me understand what was realistic and what was not—making 15 percent annualized returns with very little risk was unrealistic then and remains so today. I found out the hard way that the higher the potential returns, the higher the risk. The more illiquid the investment, the harder it is to succeed and get a return on your capital.

I realized two important things through these early experiences: (1) Market timing and stock selection are very difficult, if not impossible, to outperform over the long-term, and (2) I do not like losing money.

I realized I had to control the risks in an investment. Managing risk directly was the key to long-term success. That requires isolating all of the investment variables and determining what risk you should accept and what you should get rid of. Investors also need to understand how the investment landscape has been slowly and steadily changing beneath their feet. However, they don't generally get strategies that directly manage risk from the products and strategies pitched by this multibillion-dollar industry. Let's look at the typical strategy options and examine why I believe they continue to repeat the failures of the past.

## Modern Portfolio Theory—Not So Modern

Famed American economist Harry Markowitz, while a graduate student at the University of Chicago, developed and published the Modern Portfolio Theory (MPT) in 1952.[1] Sixty-six years later, it remains the industry standard for constructing a portfolio—the only thing I can think of that's over sixty-five and still considered "modern." MPT proposes that an investor should only choose assets that provide an optimal portfolio, which generates the best return for the least amount of risk. The most common approach to constructing this optimal portfolio uses diversification by asset allocation—seeking to balance risk among various assets within the portfolio, achieve a desired risk/return trade-off, and meet a financial goal.

Diversification is essentially spreading your money among different asset classes with the goal of minimizing the negative impact of volatility on your investments. Financial professionals implement diversification in several ways. They use different asset classes, such as stocks, bonds, real estate, gold, cash, and so on, and also diversify within the asset classes. Stocks, also called equities, can be broken into small-, mid-, or large-cap and then further divided into growth or value. Ideally, assets should be uncorrelated, i.e., when one asset goes down, another goes up. Multiple uncorrelated or offsetting investments within a portfolio balance the risk that all of your investments will decline at the same time. Diversification and asset allocation are sound concepts; in fact, I believe one should diversify, but diversification alone is not enough. It's how one diversifies and then seeks protection from market risk that matters.

Historically, the finance industry advocated for diversification as the preferred way to mitigate risk. During the 2008 Financial Crisis, however, this technique didn't perform as expected. First, many investors pursued false diversification—slicing up the market into smaller and smaller pieces instead of looking for truly uncorrelated assets to offset losses. Initially, equity markets were divided into large- and small-cap stocks before adding in the value and growth distinctions. Then, the equity markets began to split hairs with further divisions: mega-cap, micro-cap, deep value, momentum growth, and more. But none of these styles were truly new assets, just smaller slices of the same pie.

──────── Figure 5.1. How False Diversification Lurks in Modern Portfolios ────────

Source: Swan Global Investments

Investors diversifying with these assets probably felt great when the markets were going up. But the simple and neglected truth is that if everything is going up together, it will most likely all go down together, too. And that's what ended up happening.

——— Figure 5.2. Correlation Within an Asset Class, January 2005–July 2018 ———

| | 1 | 2 | 3 | 4 | 5 | 6 | 7 | 8 | 9 | 10 | 11 | 12 |
|---|---|---|---|---|---|---|---|---|---|---|---|---|
| Russell Top 200 | 1.00 | 0.96 | 0.95 | 0.92 | 0.90 | 0.87 | 0.84 | 0.85 | 0.78 | 0.80 | 0.81 | 0.75 |
| Russell Top 200 Growth | 0.96 | 1.00 | 0.82 | 0.86 | 0.91 | 0.76 | 0.78 | 0.84 | 0.67 | 0.74 | 0.79 | 0.65 |
| Russell Top 200 Value | 0.95 | 0.82 | 1.00 | 0.89 | 0.80 | 0.91 | 0.84 | 0.79 | 0.84 | 0.80 | 0.76 | 0.80 |
| Russell Midcap | 0.92 | 0.86 | 0.89 | 1.00 | 0.95 | 0.97 | 0.95 | 0.94 | 0.90 | 0.90 | 0.89 | 0.87 |
| Russell Midcap Growth | 0.90 | 0.91 | 0.80 | 0.95 | 1.00 | 0.83 | 0.89 | 0.95 | 0.78 | 0.85 | 0.90 | 0.76 |
| Russell Midcap Value | 0.87 | 0.76 | 0.91 | 0.97 | 0.83 | 1.00 | 0.92 | 0.86 | 0.94 | 0.88 | 0.82 | 0.89 |
| Russell 2000 | 0.84 | 0.78 | 0.84 | 0.95 | 0.89 | 0.92 | 1.00 | 0.97 | 0.97 | 0.98 | 0.95 | 0.96 |
| Russell 2000 Growth | 0.85 | 0.84 | 0.79 | 0.94 | 0.95 | 0.86 | 0.97 | 1.00 | 0.89 | 0.95 | 0.97 | 0.88 |
| Russell 2000 Value | 0.78 | 0.67 | 0.84 | 0.90 | 0.78 | 0.94 | 0.97 | 0.89 | 1.00 | 0.95 | 0.87 | 0.98 |
| Russell Microcap | 0.80 | 0.74 | 0.80 | 0.90 | 0.85 | 0.88 | 0.98 | 0.95 | 0.95 | 1.00 | 0.97 | 0.97 |
| Russell Microcap Growth | 0.81 | 0.79 | 0.76 | 0.89 | 0.90 | 0.82 | 0.95 | 0.97 | 0.87 | 0.97 | 1.00 | 0.90 |
| Russell Microcap Value | 0.75 | 0.65 | 0.80 | 0.87 | 0.76 | 0.89 | 0.96 | 0.88 | 0.98 | 0.97 | 0.90 | 1.00 |

| Less than 0.75 |
| Between 0.75 and 0.90 |
| Over 0.90 |

Source: Zephyr StyleADVISOR

Figure 5.2 shows how closely correlated many of these asset class "slices" or divisions of the market are. When two different assets show a correlation number close to 1, it signals that those particular assets move close to the same direction and proportion. There are a lot of 0.90s or higher in this table, reflecting high correlations of these various equity asset class slices from January 2005 through July 2018. Again, if everything goes up at the same time, it indicates that those elements will likely go down at the same time. This doesn't make a diversified portfolio. Unfortunately, many who practice this style of investing think they are truly diversified; instead, they end up with false diversification in their portfolios.

Other investors diversified by broadening their asset type exposure. They balanced their funds across international stocks, emerging market stocks, high-yield bonds, real estate, and commodities. Unfortunately, these also took a plunge during the 2008 Crisis. Just when they needed the

protection of diversification the most, it wasn't there—correlations went
straight up.

— **Figure 5.3. Correlations Among Asset Classes During the 2008 Financial Crisis** —

|  | 1 | 2 | 3 | 4 | 5 | 6 |
|---|---|---|---|---|---|---|
| 1) Russell 3000 | 1.00 | 0.92 | 0.83 | 0.75 | 0.86 | 0.59 |
| 2) MSCI EAFE Index | 0.92 | 1.00 | 0.94 | 0.73 | 0.74 | 0.63 |
| 3) MSCI Emerging Markets | 0.83 | 0.94 | 1.00 | 0.75 | 0.62 | 0.69 |
| 4) Barclays U.S. Corp High Yield | 0.75 | 0.73 | 0.75 | 1.00 | 0.70 | 0.50 |
| 5) FTSE Nareit All REITs (Real Estate) | 0.86 | 0.74 | 0.62 | 0.70 | 1.00 | 0.41 |
| 6) S&P GSCI (GS Commodity Index) | 0.59 | 0.63 | 0.69 | 0.50 | 0.41 | 1.00 |

☐ Less than 0.49               ▨ Between 0.80 and 0.89
*Source: Zephyr StyleADVISOR;*    ☐ Between 0.50 and 0.69        ■ Over 0.90
*Swan Global Investments*         ▨ Between 0.70 and 0.79

For diversification to truly work, assets need to have different return
patterns and low, ideally negative, correlation numbers. A truly uncorrelated asset has very high certainty of acting differently, not because it has
in the past, but because it is built to do so. Yet MPT is built entirely on the
backward-looking, historical assumptions of risk, return, and correlation.
Unfortunately, history doesn't always repeat itself and when correlation or
risk/return fails to match the past, portfolios can be devastated. It's hard to
manage the road ahead if you're simply looking backwards.

## Portfolio Construction

Bonds and equities make up the vast majority of portfolios. The typical
allocation is 60 percent equities and 40 percent bonds. Periodic rebalancing maintains this ratio; if an asset class becomes a too-large piece of
the pie, then the proportion of stocks to bonds is typically adjusted over
time depending on age and risk tolerance. The equity portion is meant to
grow and appreciate investors' wealth. The bond portion—the safer, more
conservative percentage—should offset market risk and reduce volatility.

It should also provide some income, relative to the yield of the bonds, in the form of regular coupon payments. If a bear market in equities shows up or a spike of volatility shakes the markets, the assumption (hope) is that bonds will anchor the portfolio so it doesn't lose as much overall, and vice versa.

Many experts consider a traditional 60/40 portfolio to be the benchmark diversified solution in portfolio management. The term 60/40 has become shorthand for a balanced portfolio, a standard allocation offering just the right amount of risk for investors to reach a targeted return (usually between 6 percent and 8 percent per year). And for a generation, the mix worked well. Equities provided capital appreciation while bonds provided some capital appreciation and some income or yield along the way.

In past markets, the 40 percent in fixed income may have provided some shelter and non-correlated returns, but thanks to today's incredibly low interest rate environment, it will not likely deliver its historical performance going forward. Remember: Bond values and interest rates have an inverse correlation, so when interest rates rise, bond values fall and vice versa.

In the next major bear market, equity and fixed income could move down in tandem, devastating a large portion of portfolio values and failing to protect investors' wealth. Those nearing retirement who have traditionally increased their fixed-income allocation may see even larger declines. Renowned bond manager Bill Gross put it this way: "The bond market's 7.5 percent forty-year historical return is just that—history. In order to duplicate that number, yields would have to drop to -17 percent!"[2] In other words, investors, you ain't going to get much from the 40 percent going forward—certainly nothing like what you got during the past forty years.

## Equities

At the time of this writing, equities are still in bull market (growth and expansion) territory—the second longest in history. Early 2018 saw some rough patches before settling a bit. But then on Christmas Eve, the market sold off and bottomed out, resulting in the worst December since 1931. Not only was this a negative year for stocks, it was the first year where all major asset classes underperformed cash since 1984. The drop in the last quarter of 2018 was -19.36% from peak to trough and cannot be classified as a bear market (losses of 20 percent or more from a market high) from a numerical perspective. We have not seen a serious, long-lasting bear market (contraction) since the 2008 financial crisis.

According to Bank of America Merrill Lynch research, there have been twenty-five bull markets in the United States since 1929. The average bull market lasts 30.7 months and the market is up 103.5 percent during that span. However, that average has been heavily skewed by the record-long bull market that lasted from late 1987 to early 2000. If one looks at the median bull market, it lasts just over thirteen months and is up roughly 73.1 percent over that span. As of September 2018, the current bull market has been going for 115 months and has been up almost 384 percent from the bottom. Bank of America Merrill Lynch research also reports that, on average, bear markets occur every 3.7 years, last about 10 months, erase more than 35 percent of the market's value and require about 3.3 years to recover. No one is sure when this bull market will end. It might be weeks, months, or years, but there have been rumblings of a bear market appearing in 2019 or possibly 2020.

Since the 1980s, the bull markets have been longer and the bear markets more severe than the historical averages going back to 1929. Government and central bank intervention have lengthened both. In the bear market of 2001–02, the S&P 500 lost more than 43 percent on an annual basis. In 2008 the S&P 500 lost 37 percent on an annual basis. In the name of stimulating consumption—pushing interest rates low and keeping them there, while printing money and expanding federal balance sheets by buying bonds—the SGRs created incentives to invest in risk assets. Why would someone hold money in a savings account paying less than a fraction of a percent, when inflation more than erodes that meager interest? So money flows to riskier assets, pushing values higher and higher.

Equity markets are vulnerable to big losses due to market risk. Market risk brought markets down to their 40 percent and 50 percent levels, on a monthly basis, during the 2008 Crisis, shocking investors. By definition, market risk cannot be diversified, yet MPT holds that diversification is the best way to manage risk. Diversification may mediate business and credit risk, but it cannot prevent the unpredictable, life-altering market corrections that can take years for people to recover from.

## Bonds

One can debate the economic impact of the Federal Reserve's decisions to force interest rates to historically low levels and then inject massive amounts of liquidity (through the purchase of bonds of various types in record amounts) into the financial system. The real-world impact on savers and investors, however, has been unarguably catastrophic. Once upon a time, managing a pension plan was simple: You'd set up a combination of dividend-paying, blue chip stocks and investment grade bonds and your work was over. Meanwhile, retirees could put their life savings into bonds and live off the interest. Those days are long gone.

Since the defeat of high inflation in the late 1970s, bonds have been a terrific investment. As every investor should know, bond yield and bond prices are inversely related. As bond yields fell from double-digit levels to their current lows, the Barclays U.S. Aggregate Bond Index gained an average of 8 percent per year, as you can see in Figure 5.4. The dark line charts this growth in 10-year Treasury values while the lighter grey line shows the decline of the yield on the 10-year Treasury bonds over that time period.

——————— **Figure 5.4. Decades-long Bull Market in Bonds as Yields Fell** ———————

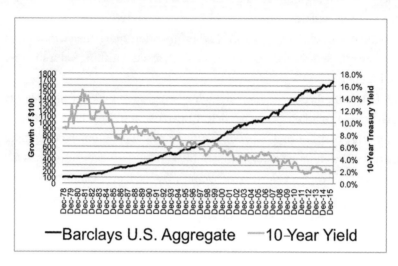

*Source: Zephyr StyleADVISOR; Swan Global Investments*

Such returns have likely met the actuarial needs of many portfolios. However, there is simply not enough gas in the tank now—the likelihood of future bond returns looking anything close to the historical returns is very small.

Historically, fixed income performed a dual role in investor portfolios: capital preservation and income. These days, investors have to choose one or the other. Starved for yield, investors have been taking on more risk. In pursuit of higher yields, money has flooded to "spread" products—high-yield bonds, foreign bonds, emerging market debt, bank loan products—anything that promises to deliver some kind of income or decent yield.

Unfortunately, savers can no longer have their cake and eat it too. By chasing yield, they have put their capital at higher risk. Usually, if an investment has a higher yield, it takes on more credit risk (the likelihood of default). During the last market correction, that didn't work out so well. Figure 5.5 illustrates how average mutual funds in various fixed-income asset classes performed during the 2008 Crisis.

— **Figure 5.5. Spread Bonds During Financial Crisis, October 2007-February 2009** —

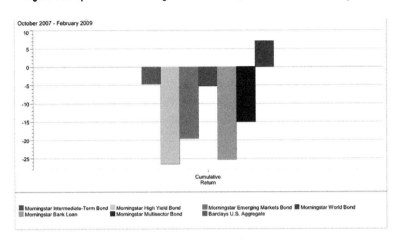

Source: Zephyr StyleADVISOR

Many investors endured significant losses last time. Those products with the lowest credit quality performed the worst (high-yield, bank loans, emerging market debt). I would argue the stage is set for even worse performances by these types of investments the next time things get ugly. Take this past year, 2018, for example. It was the first year since 1969 where both stocks and the US 10-year treasury were negative in the same year. Will bonds be able to manage risk the same way they have in the past?

## Is the 60/40 Portfolio Broken?

With the current bond and equities markets, investors have a dual dilemma. Do they flock to riskier investments for yield and sacrifice protection from the next bear market? Or do they stick to their more conservative investments, losing out on the monumental gains of this raging bull market? Simply put: Given the economic, political, social, and financial headwinds we are facing, it is grossly unrealistic to expect the kind of returns we have seen from the 60/40 portfolio over the last several decades going forward.

Academic researchers often theorize that the market will return some number based on just the right amount of risk one can tolerate. As a start-ing point for their numbers, however, they use historical data going back before the Great Depression. The 1930s and '40s have little relevance in today's world, which looks very different. The rate of change is accelerating. Global markets are vastly different and more interconnected and interde-pendent, not to mention carrying historic levels of debt. So we should be looking forward for what to do, not to eighty years ago—another reason to challenge and change the MPT.

I'm not the only one with a grim outlook for future stock and bond mar-ket returns. Figure 5.6 summarizes an audit we conducted at Swan Global Investments in an attempt to find some consensus forecasts for equity and fixed income. On the equity side, the various models factored in things like earnings growth, profitability, share buy-backs, dividends, and the like. Fixed-income forecasts were typically made using current Treasury yields, adding a risk premium for various spread products. Regardless of the methodology used, most experts predicted equity returns in the low- to mid-single digits, and fixed-income returns a few hundred basis points lower. Figure 5.6 shows forecasts by leaders in the industry. Their forecasts are for the next ten years.

The bullish predictions for stocks and bonds we found came from an audit of public defined benefit plans. According to a February 2016 National Association of State Retirement Administrators study, the stated median expected return for their balanced portfolios was 7.62 percent annualized. Looking at the table of experts, I don't know how one will possibly be able to mix and match the numbers in the stocks and bonds columns and expect to get results close to 7.62 percent. To me, it looks like another example of kicking the can down the road.

## Figure 5.6. What the Experts Say

| Source | Organization | Equities | Bonds |
|---|---|---|---|
| Vanguard Group[3] | Vanguard Group | 4.0% | 3.0% |
| BlackRock[4] | BlackRock | 3.6% | 1.8% |
| Rob Arnott[5] | Research Affiliates | 0.4% | 2.8% |
| J.P. Morgan[6] | J.P. Morgan Asset Management | 5.5% | 2.5% |
| Morningstar Investment Management[7] | Morningstar | 1.8% | 2.5% |
| "Long-Term Asset Class Forecasts"[8] | State Street Global Advisors | 6.36% | 3.7% |
| "Ten-Year Capital Market Assumptions"[9] | BNY Mellon Investment Management | 6.3% | 2.6% |

*Source: Swan Global Investments*

To understand how unrealistic current return expectations are, consider the following example. Take a simple 60 percent stock/40 percent bond portfolio. Assume that the bond portion gives us a 2 percent real return after discounting inflation (which might be an overly generous estimate). If we needed to generate a total return of 8 percent from the portfolio, what would the remaining 60 percent have to generate for us to hit that target?

## Figure 5.7. Necessary Fixed Income and Equity Returns for Desired Total Portfolio Return

| Fixed Income | | | Equity | | | Total Portfolio |
|---|---|---|---|---|---|---|
| Weight | Yield | Return | Weight | Equity Return | Return | |
| 40% | 2.0% | 0.8% | 60% | 8.67% | 5.2% | 6.0% |
| 40% | 2.0% | 0.8% | 60% | 10.33% | 6.2% | 7.0% |
| 40% | 2.0% | 0.8% | 60% | 12.00% | 7.2% | 8.0% |
| 40% | 2.0% | 0.8% | 60% | 13.67% | 8.2% | 9.0% |
| 40% | 2.0% | 0.8% | 60% | 15.33% | 9.2% | 10.0% |

*Source: Swan Global Investments*

The answer, as seen in Figure 5.7, is 12 percent. Simple algebra tells us that the 60 percent portion in equities would have to generate 12 percent to overcome the dead weight of bonds and achieve an 8 percent target return. Given the fact that returns of this magnitude are highly unlikely, the individual investor faces a dismal set of options:

• Save more.

• Work longer and postpone retirement.

• Ratchet up the risk in the portfolio and hope it works out.

• Lower expected returns.

• Try to reduce anticipated spending rates post-retirement.

Now, which one would you realistically take on?

During the 2008 Crisis, many portfolios that followed the 60/40 model failed to offer investors the necessary protection. A traditional 60/40 portfolio was down 32.54 percent from 2007 to 2009. And yet here we are, ten years later. Most investors are still doing the same thing at the urging of their advisors and for fear of doing anything differently. We are nine-plus years into a bull market, and people can be shortsighted. Instead of questioning the current model and asking what can be done differently, they chase returns and put off risk management until they need it. But by then, it could be too late.

## The Risk That Really Hurts

Most investors think of risk in terms of the amount of money they may lose, and therefore, their biggest concern is capital preservation. The industry, on the other hand, looks at and measures risk using standard deviation, more commonly referred to as volatility. Standard deviation measures the size of up or down moves in value. One would doubt that many financial advisors fielded calls from angry clients in 2008 and 2009 asking, "What was my volatility last month?" It's likely that most asked, "How much money did I lose?" Yet the traditional measure of risk, which supports traditional ways of building a portfolio and Modern Portfolio Theory, is out of step with what matters most to investors. Those who take a purely traditional approach run the risk not only of being out of touch with the primary concern of investors, but also of not adjusting their portfolio construction methods. This could lead to a repeat of past failures to protect portfolios from major losses.

We frequently sit in rooms with smart and experienced people who tell us they can combine hundreds of strategies and control the risk with precision. While they believe they really know investment strategy, markets may change. Their strategy may not adjust consistently with those market changes. These otherwise smart people essentially do the same things, but expect performance in times of major market stress to be different, though there is no evidence to support that prospect—I'd call that fiduciary insanity. It goes back to my thesis about the limits of diversification: You cannot count on it to work all the time. Unfortunately, the time you need it most is when it probably works the least.

If I am certain of one thing, it's that you cannot control human beings. Diversification and passive buy-and-hold strategies are meant to protect investors. But as we've seen in the past, investors are often their own worst enemies. For the last four decades, Dalbar Inc.'s annual research report on investor behavior has repeatedly demonstrated this.[10] Investors tend to sell at a low due to a strong aversion to losing more money than they've already lost. The long-term results are worse than if they had just clenched their teeth and rode it out. The research also shows investors tend to chase returns, buying at a high, because they don't want to miss the party and the gains. You don't have to look beyond the current lengthy bull market to see this. Despite this late stage, people are still buying. If diversification can't protect investors from selling at lows and cashing out during a bear market, is it really that effective? Portfolio construction, therefore, needs to be redefined.

The best way to counter the weaknesses in MPT and diversification is to directly address what they can't: market risk. As I've stated earlier, market risk can't be diversified away. But it can be hedged away. What does this mean? This means a redefinition of the portfolio pie is necessary to best position investors to achieve their desired outcomes in this rapidly changing world: a well-diversified portfolio across many asset classes that also addresses MPT's Achilles' heel by hedging market risk.

Hedging is the missing piece to making a diversified portfolio work the way it should. I believe it's the only way to prepare for the inevitable consequences of a current political and economic system fraught with overspending and overreach. Because what goes up must come down.

6

# HEDGED EQUITY:
# REDEFINING THE PORTFOLIO PIE

The current risk in the markets is quite high, but this risk cannot be eliminated through traditional approaches to portfolio construction, nor by timing or modeling (picking particular investments). This is a unique time in history where interventionism can cause markets to behave irrationally for long periods of time. We have not been here on this scale before, ever. Of course, many recessions/depressions have occurred over the course of our country's history and around the world but not on the truly global scale that can occur in today's interconnected economy. As detailed earlier, never before have the world's economies been so intertwined and in debt.

The Smartest Guys in the Room (SGRs) around the globe have pushed the envelope and gone all in to try to keep the proverbial party going. No one wants to take away the spiked punch bowl. But the longer that punch bowl is out, the bigger the hangover will eventually be.

We are already seeing behavior that would ordinarily be deemed irrational. Approximately 30 percent of all sovereign bonds have negative rates, just shy of $10 trillion as of June 2017. Rational investors should never, ever, ever lend money to an entity that is irresponsible, let alone entertain the idea of paying for the privilege to do so! Even if a country seems semi-responsible, or at least perhaps not in as much trouble as Italy or Spain from a fiscal standpoint, a rational investor should never consider an investment that guarantees a loss over its lifetime. The conclusion should be that today's central banks, governments (one of the biggest "buyers" of these negative yielding investments), and investors are anything but rational. Governments and central bankers now have to work closely together to try to avoid the disaster that is approaching.

And while Modern Portfolio Theory (MPT) is part of the solution, it is not the entire solution. Adding another layer of risk control, by hedging the portfolio, improves the probabilities of success.

Hedged equity is essentially as simple as it sounds: One invests in an equity investment and then overlays some sort of hedging strategy to that equity investment. The concept is simple, but successfully executing a hedging strategy over time and in various markets is not. Let's dive into the various ways hedged equity can benefit investors and help redefine their portfolios to appropriately address the challenges they face today and going forward.

## Seeking a Better Buy-and-Hold

Investors need to be invested for growth. But the often-wild ride of equity markets can be a difficult one for many investors to stomach. Thinking you can time the market and get out right before it drops is a lost cause, in my opinion. It is too hard to do this consistently enough to make it a proper form of risk management. And even if you can get out in time, when do you get back in? You could miss out on significant gains if you re-enter the market just a month after it begins picking up again.

Many investors already know this. The current trend in investing is the passive buy-and-hold—it's all the rage. With the rise of index funds, exchange-traded funds (ETFs), and robo-advisors, investing is much easier, less time consuming, and more available. While this approach can deliver returns in a raging bull market, it gets tested when problems eventually arise during a financial or market crisis. That's what matters most—how well do people buy and hold when the ride gets bumpy? Well, as Dalbar Inc.[1] and many other researchers, including the 2017 Nobel laureate in economic sciences, Richard H. Thaler,[2] have shown, not very well.

Loss aversion, or the fear of losing, is such a strong emotional reaction that the moment people start seeing red on their statements, many start hitting the eject button instead of holding through the fall. Again, this behavior often worsens the blow. Large losses can be incredibly painful in the short term and result in people getting out of the market completely, but even more dramatic is the impact on the long-term success of investment returns. Many studies show the value of avoiding large losses, as well as how behavioral bias contributes to people continually and frequently participating in large losses. The industry knows this research, and yet it hasn't really offered a solution.

Low-cost, passive investing doesn't address these investors' greatest fear: losing money. It only makes the bumpy roller-coaster ride of the markets cheaper to buy. In effect, making risk less expensive may actually diminish investors' focus on risk, thereby replacing risk management with fee management. The main problem with buy-and-hold is that it doesn't address investor behavior during a bumpy or volatile ride. Too often, buy-and-hold becomes buy-and-fold. So I set out to smooth the ride in order to create a better buy-and-hold.

A hedged equity approach allows you to always be passively invested for long-term growth while having some protection in place against the major losses that often plague passive investors. Hedging allows you to address market risk directly. Mitigating market risk helps investors lose less, and by losing less they can gain more in the end. How? It's all about the math. And math matters.

## Math Matters

Many investor decisions are driven by fear and greed. They forget that investing is a math game, and it is math that delivers the results. Almost all investors know the significance and power of compounding in their investments. While this is a fantastic mathematical force when the market is going up, people forget that compounding also works in reverse when the market is going down.

I noted in Chapter 4 that the more money you lose, the more you need to break even. One really bad year can undo years of gains. Large losses are incredibly painful in the short term but even more so on the long-term success of investment returns. As the "Oracle of Omaha," Warren Buffett, once said: "It takes twenty years to build a reputation and five minutes to ruin it. If you think about that, you'll do things differently." You could replace the word "reputation" with "portfolio," since large losses can quickly and disastrously wipe out years of investment growth. With that in mind, you *should* do things differently and always address and define risk in such a way that large losses do not occur, or at least occur less frequently. For example, a solid 8 percent a year means you can double your money in nine years (rule of 72). But if you take a 50 percent loss in year ten, you would be right back to where you started and the annualized return over those years would be zero percent.

You've heard the phrase "less is more." This can certainly be true with investing. The math behind investment returns dictates that even if you participate in fewer of the upside moves of the market, as long as you participate in fewer of the downside moves, as well, you stand to gain more over time than if you simply were to buy and hold and ride the markets all the way up and down.

If you were somehow able to miraculously avoid any participation during months when the stock market was down overall, you would only need to capture about 26 percent of the gains during the up months to match the overall performance of the market over that time (9.48 percent annualized return for the Dow Jones Industrial Average Total Return or 9.47 percent for the S&P 500 Total Return). If your participation in the down months was 40 percent, then you would need to capture 55 percent in the up months to match the market. This comes as an astonishing realization to most investors—a definite reason to rethink the math behind investments. So many investors fall into the bad habit of hopping from one investment to another, trying to "beat the market." It's like changing lanes in rush hour traffic. It always seems like you're making progress, until that car you were in front of three minutes ago passes you. Similarly, the key to successful long-term investing is minimizing or avoiding losses so you can accomplish your long-term financial goal on time, not simply trying to find the hottest performer to get great up-market participation!

How big of a difference can avoiding large losses make over the long term? The following illustration demonstrates the amazing impact of loss avoidance compared to a buy-and-hold strategy.

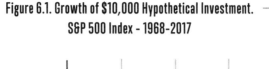

Figure 6.1. Growth of $10,000 Hypothetical Investment.
S&P 500 Index - 1968-2017

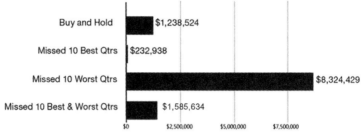

*Source: Swan Global Investments, Morningstar. Based on the S&P 500 Index returns from January 1968 through December 2017.*

A $10,000 investment in the S&P 500 Index in 1968, if left alone, would have grow to an astounding $1.238 million by the end of 2017 (12,380 percent). However, avoiding the ten worst quarters in the index across the two hundred quarters for that time period would result in 572 percent more capital or $8.324 million (83,240 percent compared to 12,380 percent)!

Avoiding periods of large decline can have an enormous impact on returns (and peace of mind). Although it is statistically impossible for any equity strategy to completely avoid all of the worst quarters in the market over a long time frame, it is possible, through proper hedging or other various strategies, to miss out on some of the downside associated with the worst performing quarters in the market. Thus, in essence, an investor can "miss" some of those quarters. Even if this means missing out on full participation in some of the best quarters, missing the worst quarters has a much greater effect on an investor's bottom line. If all of the worst and best quarters were completely missed, an investor still ends up with an amount

35 percent higher than a purely passive buy-and-hold approach ($1.585 million). This is due to the power of compounding and avoiding the power of negative compounding.

Not only can hedging against major losses reduce the recovery time when the markets fall 30 percent or 40 percent, but equally important, by doing so, such an approach gives investors a smoother ride. They are more likely to remain invested, avoid emotional reactions, and stay on track to meeting the long-term goals they planned with their advisors. After all, the best financial plan is only as good as the investor's ability to stick with it.

## Hedging Shouldn't Be an Ugly Word

What comes to mind when you hear the word "hedge"? Hedge funds? Scandals? High risk? Leverage? Fraud? Hedging may have a bad reputation, but wrongfully so. Hedging doesn't need to be synonymous with hedge funds, but it is in the minds of many. So let's take a closer look at hedging.

Initially, hedge funds had the purpose of doing what the term actually means: to protect against loss while seeking gains. Now, hedge funds' bad reputation often stems from the practice of taking riskier positions to increase gains by combining hedging with betting on winners and losers, while often including leverage (borrowing money to place market bets), like Long-Term Capital Management did in the 1990s.

Hedging in and of itself does *not* equal hedge fund. Often, the purposes of the two are at odds with one another. Typically, one hedges to reduce the negative effects of market risk and volatility in a portfolio. The hedge is intended to offset potential losses by transferring risk in various ways, such as options, short selling, or futures contracts. The goal is to lose less money in your investments, especially during times of major market stress. If your portfolio spends less time recovering, it can spend more time compounding.

Hedging has been around a long time. Farmers, airlines, insurance firms, corporations, banks—they all hedge to manage the biggest risks in their businesses. Farmers hedge against changes in seed, livestock, and crop prices. Airlines hedge against big changes in oil prices. Banks hedge against interest rate risk. If you have car or home insurance, you are essentially hedging against potential property loss either due to a car accident or housing catastrophe.

On some level, diversifying your portfolio can also be considered a form of hedging. The idea of spreading your money across many investments is like hedging your bets versus putting all of your money in one investment, as well as hoping the different investments you select in a portfolio offset one another. For example, many investors buy bonds to offset potential losses in stocks with the expectation that bonds and stocks are uncorrelated and won't move in the same direction at the same time. This, however, hasn't always been the case, as I pointed out in the previous chapter. During the 2008 Financial Crisis, many types of bond funds lost value at the same time as nearly every category of stocks. Diversification alone isn't enough to manage market risk—so why not couple it with a hedging strategy?

Some common ways to hedge, or minimize risk and offset losses, include market timing, short selling, futures contracts, and options. Market timing and short selling depend on one's ability to successfully and repeatedly predict the market. As I've stated, it is difficult to consistently time when to buy or sell across all holdings in a portfolio over and over, year after year, making this approach an undependable risk management approach. My strategy depends on a different hedging tool: put options.

## Hedging with Put Options

The key to a hedging strategy is to take an uncorrelated offsetting position relative to some asset (stock, etc.). A put option is an option contract giving the owner the right, but not the obligation, to sell a specified amount of an underlying security at a specified price within a specified time frame.[3] As such, there is an opportunity for investors to use a put option to hedge against future price changes. Put options on an asset are especially effective for hedging since a put option is inversely correlated to the asset itself, therefore providing both the offsetting of risk and non-correlation one desires when seeking diversification. For example, when you use a put option on a stock, if the stock price goes down, the value of the put option goes up, and vice versa. For more on put options, see Appendix 1.

Put options are much more effective in managing and reducing risk than other forms of hedging. They offer control over the hedging process, are inversely correlated to assets they seek to protect, offer flexibility within the contract period, may reduce adverse investor behavior, and offer profit potential.

## Control

Options allow you to define and limit the amount of risk you are willing to take over a specified time frame. In other words, they allow you to quantify how much you are willing to lose. This kind of control is an advantage that market timing and diversification strategies lack. Market timing as a hedging approach relies on forecasting what the market will do, but you can't control or predict markets, so this approach is impractical for risk control. Market timing provides only the illusion of control when managers assume they can effectively call the tops or bottoms of markets at just the right time. The illusion is exposed when managers get it wrong, potentially costing their clients a lot of money. Similarly, as outlined in the MPT section of Chapter 5, diversification often creates a false sense of security since it depends on asset classes being uncorrelated in all market conditions.

## Correlation

For an effective diversification strategy, the offset position needs to be inversely correlated with the underlying asset. If assets are highly correlated, there is limited protection in place against big market sell-offs. When the 2008 Financial Crisis occurred, many asset classes became highly correlated and sold off in unison; thus, diversification failed to protect the portfolio as certain theories promised. Put options, on the other hand, are always inversely correlated, based on the nature of the option contract itself, and thus are a more reliable hedge position than asset allocation alone. Again, when the underlying value goes down, the put option value goes up and vice versa.

### Investor Behavior

Used correctly, put options may help investors avoid making damaging investment decisions in a volatile environment. When portfolios are losing money, despite managers' and advisors' best intentions and advice, investors tend to panic and sell at a low. Market timing and diversification are especially sensitive to emotional decision making, so using a hedge approach that minimizes negative impact of investor behavior is paramount.

The effective use of put options may help smooth out a portfolio's return by minimizing the amount of loss in times of market stress, thus helping to ease the emotional roller-coaster ride for investors. Put options directly address market risk, as well as investor behavior that may be detrimental to long-term investing success.

## Win by Not Losing

Many investors are unfamiliar with options—and the unfamiliar can cause apprehension or avoidance. Some may shy away from mutual funds or other investments that use options due to unfamiliarity with options or their capabilities. However, given the changing world and its likely ramifications, investors need other options (pun intended) to address the risks that lie ahead. Hedging a portfolio with put options offers a direct way to address market risk and gives the investor a chance to limit the damage caused by inevitable bear markets or the coming SGR-driven storm. I believe that by actively seeking to not lose big, investors will be better off in the long run. And this is what I seek to accomplish with my Defined Risk Strategy (DRS), a rules-based, time-tested, hedged equity approach that manages risk and seeks to define or limit the amount of loss on an annual basis by hedging with put options.

## Redefining the Portfolio Pie

As I outlined in Chapter 5, traditional approaches to portfolio construction relied on some diversification of investments across many asset classes, but ultimately it came down to a balance of stocks and bonds—typically some derivation of a 60/40 portfolio. Going forward, the traditional 60/40 portfolio, and derivations thereof, will be under tremendous pressure and highly unlikely to reproduce their historical returns. I believe that traditional methods will not solve the new challenges the SGRs have created. As such, the portfolio pie needs to be redefined, with different components that can effectively address these challenges. If bonds are challenged to offer portfolio protection and stocks remain prone to bear markets as natural law dictates, then hedged equity should comprise a significant portion, if not a majority, of the portfolio pie.

Here's the traditional 60/40 portfolio, again with 60 percent invested in stocks and 40 percent invested in bonds.

### Figure 6.2. Traditional 60/40 Portfolio

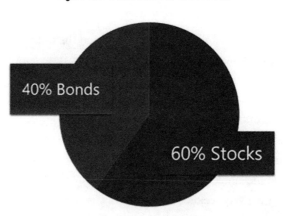

Source: *Swan Global Investments*

As I outlined in detail in Chapter 5, the bond portion of the portfolio will face more challenges going forward, either because persistently low interest rates will deliver low yield (income) from bonds or because any rise in interest rates will create a fall in the value of the bonds. The worst has yet to come for bonds. Further, we know stocks have enjoyed a protracted bull market, which will eventually end.

However, introducing hedged equity into the portfolio, either as a large allocation to the stock portion of the pie or via multiple portions of various hedged equity asset classes (e.g., hedged foreign developed equity, hedged emerging markets equity, etc.), to complement a portfolio's existing equity asset classes may provide meaningful protection, as well as upside capture. Either way, adding a significant allocation to hedged equity (too little won't make a meaningful impact) may provide the type of protection that investors will need going forward, while perhaps enabling investors to allocate more of the overall pie to equities versus bonds, given the fact bonds will likely be a drag going forward.

But the devil is in the details. It is important to note, not every hedged equity strategy is the same. Some strategies are hedged only some of the time (tactically applying hedges based on market timing). Other strategies use short-term hedging that requires consistent replacement of the hedge, which may fail to protect in long bear markets when replacing the hedge is too costly to execute. Still others only hedge a portion of the downside movement in the market, leaving investors exposed to any and all market losses beyond a predetermined amount of drawdown. I spent years carefully testing different hedging strategies given certain market conditions and analyzing those details, before settling on an always invested, always hedged approach that I believe offers investors the best probability of long-term success given the challenges ahead. I'll describe that in more detail in the next chapter.

Figure 6.3 shows a hypothetical portfolio before and after applying a hedged equity strategy, in this case the DRS, to complement each major class of equities within the portfolio: US large-cap equities, US small-cap equities, foreign developed equities, and emerging market equities. As typical portfolios may incorporate both active and passive strategies for stock and bond investments, which I've shown here, the net result is still about 60 percent stock and 40 percent bond investments.

## Figures 6.3. and 6.4. Hypothetical Portfolios: Before DRS and After DRS

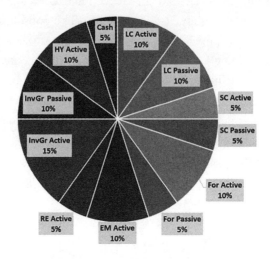

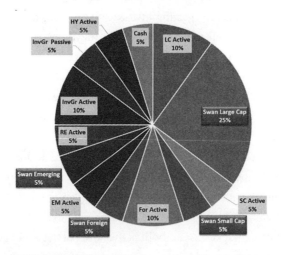

*Source: Swan Global Investments*

The investing landscape has changed, redefined by SGRs and government overreach and overspending. If the traditional approach to constructing the portfolio pie will not generate sufficient returns going forward or fails to provide sufficient protection from the next bear market, much less a major economic fallout, then the portfolio pie must change! Below is the same portfolio, however, now a significant portion of the overall pie, 40 percent in this example, is hedged, which I believe is a minimum that will be necessary going forward. That leaves the other 60 percent unhedged.

—————————————— Figure 6.5. Hypothetical Portfolio: After DRS ——————————————

DRS assets
40%

Unhedged exposure
60%

*Source: Swan Global Investments*

This is a new, redefined view of how investors should consider portfolio construction—which asset classes are used and how much of the portfolio is hedged and how much is not hedged. Further, the next considerations should be what hedging method is being used, and how it is being managed. I'll explain how I addressed these considerations and many more with a dive into the DRS in the next chapter.

# INVESTING REDEFINED: WHY THE DRS IS A BETTER SOLUTION

"The Devil is in the details, but so is salvation."
—US NAVY ADMIRAL HYMAN G. RICKOVER

The Defined Risk Strategy (DRS) is a rules-based, hedged equity (asset) strategy, designed to provide the highest possible return with the lowest amount of risk over a full market cycle. Our strategy seeks to provide the greatest probability of accomplishing long-term capital growth, while providing some downside protection along the way. I pursued this goal by designing the strategy to take into account all market outcomes and return possibilities, attach a probability to each of those possibilities, and structure an optimized return pattern given that range of market possibilities. The DRS can fulfill its goal without having to predict or time the market, without picking stocks or sectors, and without having complicated portfolio construction issues dependent on past correlation assumptions. Since 1997, the strategy has had a track record of accomplishing its goal.

I designed the DRS with the endgame in mind—it is outcome-oriented and investor-centered. Above all, I sought the best way to directly address market risk, mitigate volatility, and protect against extreme events to deliver a more predictable set of long-term investment outcomes. In the late 1990s, I saw our global economy transforming. I observed that Smartest Guys in

the Room (SGRs) intervention was leading to larger unintended consequences, thus permanently altering the investing landscape and pushing
the limits of natural law. If I was right, according to Pascal's Wager, then I
needed to devise a strategy that could address the risks of a wide range of
calamitous outcomes, including the fallout scenarios outlined in Chapter 4.
I tried many different approaches and selected the combination of strategy
components that would accomplish this objective. I knew that smoothing
out returns through market events and reducing emotional distress would
make it easier to achieve my long-term goals and to build overall financial
plans. I wasn't following the herd or convention; I built the DRS based on
what was best for investors like you and me. Finally, given my background
as a CPA, I was also very purposeful in constructing the DRS in a tax-efficient manner. Taxes have a major impact on the final realized return an
investor can achieve, and given the challenges ahead, I believe taxes are not
likely to decrease over time.

## Keeping Investors Invested–Addressing Investor Behavior

As investors, we can be our own worst enemy. When the markets are going
crazy or falling at an alarming rate and uncertainty, conjecture, and panic
are building, our emotions kick in and the only thing we want to do is hit
the eject button to preserve our capital. As I've stated before, and as the
extensive research by Shlomo Benartzi,[1] Robert Thaler,[2] Dalbar Inc.,[3] and
others clearly shows, a buy-and-hold passive strategy is much harder to
stick with in times of crisis. Selling in those moments of fear (panic selling)
will realize what was, up to that moment, only a paper loss, and then you
will also have to correctly time a reentry point. Investors often wait a long
time after panic selling, until the pain of the loss subsides, which may be
after the market has rebounded substantially. Thus, they miss out on much
of that recovery. In this way, bear markets have a very negative impact on
an investor's wealth and emotional state.

In managing investments, I view risk in two ways:

1. Absolute loss—the total amount of money an investor loses over a
   given time frame

2. Volatility—the price swings that an investment experiences

As such, our approach to risk management aligns with what most concerns investors: losing big and not having the money they need when they need it. The DRS seeks to define, or limit, risk of large losses and major price swings on an annual basis. Again, this may help investors avoid pulling out at the worst time. After all, the best investment plan is only good if the investor can stick with it through the major ups and downs of the market.

## Provides More Predictable Returns

The DRS is a full market cycle strategy. That is, it is designed to provide the greatest probability of long-term success for investors through the many full market cycles (both bull and bear market) that they will face during their lifetimes. While there is a short-term cost to defining risk in order to avoid extreme, life-altering losses, the DRS seeks to capture much of the upside movement in the market over time. The goal is to outperform the market over a full cycle. Ultimately, the DRS is trying to change the distribution of returns. Rather than having a wide band of potential outcomes, both good and bad, the DRS tries to compress the possible outcomes into a much more predictable band. Building wealth is a long-term process for most investors, so think of this like the tortoise and the hare—the DRS is the tortoise, believing slow and steady wins the race.

Many of the investment models, especially those used prior to the 2008 Crisis, assumed that investment returns occur in a nice, clean, predictable pattern known as a normal distribution. However, this was a poor assumption to make.

The terms used to describe extreme market events—black swans, hundred-year storms, tail events, etc.—imply that these types of markets should be few and far between. Sadly, the last two decades have seen more than their fair share of crises. The "Asian contagion" in 1997, the Russian default and Long-Term Capital Management crisis in 1998, the dot.com bust in 2000, the 9/11 attacks in 2001, the credit crisis in 2008, and the US debt downgrade crisis in 2011 all contradict the idea that market meltdowns are rare events.

Where did this misconception come from? The answer to this question can be traced back to the concept of a "normal" distribution. First pioneered by the brilliant German mathematician Carl Friedrich Gauss in the early 1800s, the normal, bell-shaped curve proved to have many attractive properties that fostered its use across a wide variety of disciplines. If a set of data fits a normal distribution, then all kinds of predictions and assumptions can be made about future events with a high degree of accuracy. Many market participants were seduced by the simplicity and elegance of the normal distribution.

The key phrase above, however, is "if a set of data fits a normal distribution." Unfortunately, data indicates that markets do not fit the nice, simple paradigm of a normal distribution.[4]

In Figure 7.1, we see the distribution of the S&P 500 is not symmetrical. The negative events, the so-called black swans, pull the distribution to the left. In layperson's terms, there are more chances of big moves on the left side of 0 (negative). The S&P 500 experienced more losses (left tail) of -10 percent to -18 percent and worse, than gains (right tail) of 15 percent to 18 percent or better in a given year. In statistical terms, the distribution for the S&P 500 is negatively skewed. In practical terms, it means models that assume a normal distribution of market returns tend to underestimate downside risk. In simplest terms, the chart tells us that when it rains, it pours.

────────── **Figure 7.1. Monthly Return Distribution, S&P 500, 1997–2018** ──────────

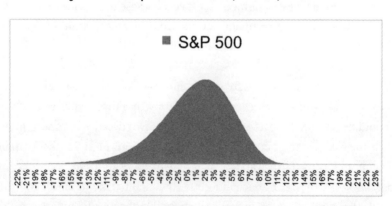

*Source: Swan Global Investments; Morningstar (smoothed monthly returns of S&P 500 Total Return for July 1997– December 2018)*

However, this type of distribution simply has too much uncertainty and downside risk for us at Swan. The goal of the DRS is to truncate as much of that left tail as possible. Sure, there will be a trade-off as part of the right tail will be sacrificed. But we are willing to trade some upside potential for downside protection. The distribution of monthly returns of the DRS is seen below.

##### Figure 7.2. Monthly Returns Distribution, DRS and S&P 500, 1997-2018

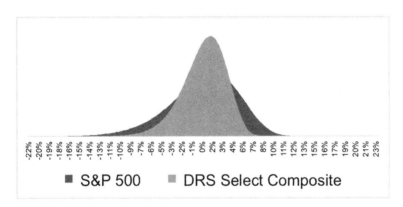

Source: Zephyr StyleADVISOR; Swan Global Investments (smoothed monthly returns of S&P 500 Total Return for July 1997– December 2018 and the DRS Select Composite). Past performance is no guarantee of future results.

Historically, we have delivered on our objective of tightening the distribution of outcomes. What this means is that by minimizing or eliminating those extreme, outlier events (like the 2008 Financial Crisis) even while sacrificing some participation in outsized gains on the upside, we get more predictable, consistent returns, which allow you to make better financial plans and have better return expectations in normal markets—and better outcomes in the event of a major economic collapse.

Figure 7.2 is based on monthly return data. With our twenty years of history, that equates to well over two hundred data points used to create the above distribution. But as I've stated numerous times, the DRS is meant to be a long-term investment vehicle and a month should not be considered long-term. So let's take a look at this with longer time frames. Figure 7.3

shows every three-year return for both the S&P 500 and the DRS between July 1997 and December 2018.

——————————— **Figure 7.3. Distribution of Rolling 3-Year Returns** ———————————

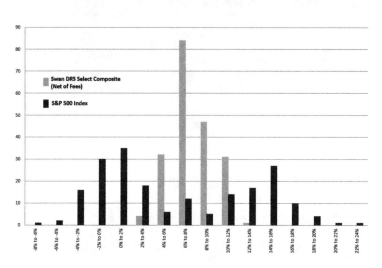

*Source: Zephyr StyleADVISOR; Swan Global Investments. The S&P 500 Index is an unmanaged index and cannot be invested into directly. Past performance is no guarantee of future results. DRS results are from the Select Composite, net of all fees, from July 1997 to December 2018.*

A plain English description of the three-year S&P 500 returns might be feast or famine. The more formal, statistical description is that this is a bimodal distribution. Usually a distribution will be clustered near the mean, or average result, and then gently slope off in both directions. However, this distribution has two or maybe even three peaks (trimodal). A large number of occurrences cluster in the 10 percent to 18 percent range, which represents a very healthy return over three years. However, there are also a large number of occurrences where the annualized three-year returns are in the -8 percent to -14 percent range. Even more interesting, while the average three-year annualized return for the S&P 500 is 5.65 percent, the index has been close to its average very few times since July 1997. In fact, the average three-year return (investor experience) was typically either way above or way below.

In contrast, by minimizing the impact of those bear markets through hedging with long-term put options, the distribution of DRS returns is what one hopes to see—the majority of three-year returns are clustered near the average of the distribution. The returns are much more predictable. The DRS doesn't have a second peak to the distribution out in negative territory, like there is for the S&P 500.

But in our view, even a three-year period is considered short-term. What do the returns over five-year or ten-year periods look like for the DRS and the S&P 500?

## Figure 7.4. Distribution of Rolling 5-Year Returns

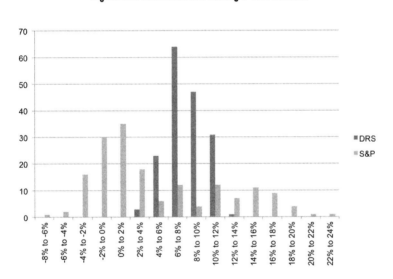

*Source: Zephyr StyleADVISOR; Swan Global Investments. The S&P 500 Index is an unmanaged index and cannot be invested into directly. Past performance is no guarantee of future results. DRS results are from the Select Composite, net of all fees, from July 1997 to December 2018.*

Compared to the S&P 500, the DRS's annualized five-year returns look very appealing. Almost two-thirds of the 169 observations occurred in the 6 percent to 10 percent range, meaning the investor averaged 6 percent to 10 percent return per year for five years. The two most common buckets for the S&P 500 were the -2 percent to 0 percent and 0 percent to 2 percent ranges. And what of the ten-year periods?

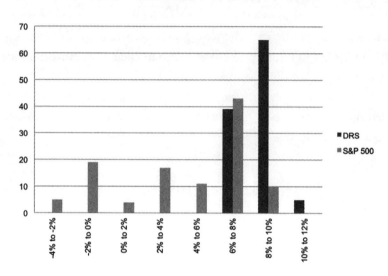

Figure 7.5. Distribution of Rolling 10-Year Returns

*Source: Zephyr StyleADVISOR; Swan Global Investments. The S&P 500 Index is an unmanaged index and cannot be invested into directly. Past performance is no guarantee of future results. DRS results are from the Select Composite, net of all fees, from July 1997 to December 2018.*

With our track record of twenty years, the sample size affords a healthy number of decade-long returns to analyze—109 observations in all. The long-term results of the DRS show a remarkable degree of consistency. Again, the value of hedging against bear market losses is powerfully illustrated in Figure 7.5.

Another key takeaway from these charts has to do with timing. At Swan we are often asked, "When is the best time to buy the DRS?" If an investor's previous market experience has been in something like the S&P 500, it is a perfectly rational question to ask. As we have seen over the last twenty years, an investor could have experienced radically different results, depending on the time frame in question. However, the DRS almost renders this question moot as the returns are consistent and therefore the range of outcomes has been tight.

## Addressing Investment Timing Risk

All investors start with the best of intentions, but nobody knows what the market will do over time. The rolling periods discussed above reflect how the DRS neutralizes investment timing risk, or the potential for different outcomes depending on when one begins their investment.

In Figure 7.6, we graph the rolling returns for twelve investors over ten-year investment periods for both the S&P 500 and the DRS. The first period runs from January 1998 to December 2007, and the last runs from January 2009 to December 2018.

The graphs powerfully illustrate how hedging can improve long-term results. Contrast the graph of the ten-year outcomes for twelve different investors in the DRS versus the experiences and outcome of those same twelve investors had they invested over the same ten-year periods in the S&P 500 instead. The anomaly that is the past ten years without a bear market is represented with the line that shoots up past $350,000.

### Figure 7.6. Seeking Consistent Outcomes

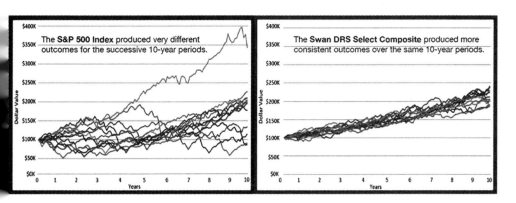

*Source: Swan Global Investments. All Swan DRS data based on historical performance of the S&P Total Return Index and the Swan DRS Select Composite. Prior performance is not a guarantee of future results.*

What these graphs don't show is the reality that many S&P investors bailed in the bear market during the 2008 Financial Crisis, taking large losses and not returning until years later. These graphs are probably the most powerful graphic expression of the goals of the DRS, its historical ability to deliver, its consistency of returns, and its capital preservation through market cycles (both bull and bear markets).

## Flexible and Adaptable

As I've stated, I created the Defined Risk Strategy to redefine the risk/return relationship of investing across multiple asset classes in my favor going forward. To accomplish those goals, I required a strategy that was flexible and adaptable to create the redefined risk/return relationship in various market conditions, applied to various asset classes. When I launched the DRS, I was only applying my investing and hedging techniques to the US large-cap equity market, as represented by the S&P 500 Index. However, the DRS is by design agnostic to the underlying asset class. It can be applied to nearly any asset with a liquid index exchange-traded fund (ETF) marketplace and a liquid corresponding options market. Over time we've applied it to other major categories of equities and other asset classes as well. Since 1997 it has been my entire solution for nearly all of my investable wealth. In other words, I eat my own cooking.

## Tax Efficiency

As I mentioned, with a CPA background, I am keenly aware of the impact of taxes on real returns and long-term wealth. Much of an investor's returns can be taken away by taxes, one way or another, either as capital gains, in the form of estate tax, or other methods. Going forward, the chances that taxes will increase are high, given the level of debt across the public sector, thanks to the SGRs. In developing the Defined Risk Strategy, I was intent on utilizing tax-efficient means to invest for growth and manage risk on the downside. So the DRS has three investment components, each of which provides tax-friendly benefits. The first component minimizes taxable events, the second carries forward losses, and the third takes advantage of long-term capital gains. I'll explore each of these tax benefits in the next chapter.

# 8

# HOW THE DEFINED RISK STRATEGY WORKS

"I've always loved to play games, and face it: Investing is one big game. You
need to be decisive, open-minded, flexible, and competitive."
—STANLEY DRUCKENMILLER, DUQUESNE CAPITAL

At Swan, we believe the Defined Risk Strategy (DRS) is the investment
solution for the volatile and uncertain environment investors face today, as
well as the daunting challenges they will face going forward. This chapter
demonstrates how the DRS works and why it is best suited to help you
reach your long-term financial goals.

As I have said, I believe that market risk, also known as systematic risk,
is the greatest threat to investors who wish to build a portfolio in the market
and that the dominant investment approaches do not sufficiently address
it. For decades, the industry has espoused Modern Portfolio Theory (MPT)
and the idea that the best form of risk management is diversification. Yet
in the same breath that theory also states that market risk cannot be diversified away.

If market risk is the single largest danger to a portfolio, why do most
strategies rely on an approach that, by definition, is insufficient? It seems
absurd to address the biggest risk in a portfolio using a strategy not up to
the job. Even as a teenager, I found the MPT insufficient during the 1987
stock market crash and the recession in 1990. I did not enjoy and could
not accept losing 25 percent to 35 percent of my portfolio during those bear

markets. Moreover, I never knew when bear markets were going to arrive or end. If I had needed access to my money during times of major drawdown, I would have further damaged my portfolio.

I needed a solution that directly addressed market risk. I further needed a solution that did not rely on timing or stock selection. I tested many ways to hedge equity, using various options strategies and underlying equity investments. Over time I settled on the process that would provide me with the highest probability of achieving the greatest long-term success through many market cycles. This solution, the DRS, was consciously constructed in light of the market conditions at the time (instability, overvaluations, unsustainable debt, and high risk, which have only become worse) and the general long-term problems that I saw building in the global interconnected economy.

Since 1997, the DRS has been tested through multiple market cycles through which it generated consistent annual returns while protecting capital from catastrophic losses, including two large bear markets (2000–02 and 2007–09, during which the S&P 500 lost -49 percent and -57 percent, respectively). The strategy has worked as designed through both down and up markets independent of the cause of those environments (political, demographic, economic). I believe this is because it assumes the occurrence of regular bear markets to be an inevitability in the investment world and not only weathers these events but capitalizes on them. As I've stated, I believe that the market will unavoidably self-correct regardless of what politicians are selling. Natural law cannot be suspended by government. My convictions aside, the DRS was designed to work through all environments. When I developed the DRS in the mid-1990s, the market outlook was optimistic, if not euphoric. Twenty years later, the outlook for both equity and bond markets is much more challenging.

If you've gotten this far with me, you must believe to some extent in a potential correction in the near future or at least agree with Pascal's Wager enough to find the need to protect yourself just in case. Because you can't remove yourself from the markets entirely (one needs to outpace inflation and grow enough wealth to live through retirement years), the Defined Risk Strategy may be something to consider to help you redefine your portfolio to address the risks we face today and beyond.

# Diving Deeper into the DRS

The Defined Risk Strategy can be applied to almost any asset or asset class (stocks, bonds, gold, real estate, etc.). We view it as an engine that can be applied to various equity assets, or as a multi-asset portfolio approach, to increase returns and lower risk over time, through full market cycles (both bull and bear markets). The DRS does not seek to sacrifice returns for the sake of protection, but rather increase returns and reduce risk over those market cycles to improve probabilities for long-term success. It is a distinct approach to address the current investment landscape and challenges ahead—investing redefined. We believe it's a better way to invest.

How can the DRS deliver both performance and protection? It is always invested and always hedged. It always maintains a buy-and-hold position in the market that makes up roughly 90 percent of the portfolio's holdings and provides upside participation with the market. The DRS addresses market risk by maintaining a hedge, using the other 10 percent of the portfolio to protect that buy-and-hold position against major market sell-offs. This always invested, always hedged position doesn't rely on market timing or stock selection or on outdated risk management solutions like MPT. Again, academia maintains that market risk cannot be diversified and therefore cannot be addressed by diversification or MPT, but it can be hedged against.

The DRS hedges with a long-term, exchange-traded put option on its underlying buy-and-hold equity position to define and limit the risk over a particular time period. The cost of the hedge is based on the market's expectation of risk. The put option is inversely correlated in large market declines. The DRS was designed specifically to address risk management first and to do so in a range of outcomes, including devastating market drawdown scenarios. This is why I've continuously made the argument that you should only choose hedges that will work in all market conditions— including a financial crisis.

Some investors view options as exotic or scary. So why does the DRS choose to use put options to implement the hedge? Why are put options a more effective form of risk management than diversification? Because smart investors have accepted options as commonplace and useful tools in risk management. For those of you who find options scary, I highly recommend referencing Appendix 1, where I discuss the nature and evolution of the options marketplace. The objective of the appendix is to help you understand what options are and the benefits they can bring to a portfolio. Readers who know options can be used as a risk management tool can proceed directly to the next section, where we discuss the role options play in the DRS.

## How the DRS Works

The DRS is composed of three separate but complementary components: invest in equities, create a hedged position, and collect option premium through market-neutral trading strategies. We believe this process to be transparent, disciplined, and most important, repeatable. Let's look at each component in turn.

### 1. Equity Component

The DRS starts off with a core buy-and-hold position in a market. That position is established and maintained via passive investments in broad, index-based exchange-traded funds (ETFs) that make up the vast majority of the portfolio's holdings, typically 85 percent to 90 percent of the portfolio. We incorporate this buy-and-hold approach via ETFs for two reasons.

First, we believe investors need to always be invested for the growth potential and capital appreciation provided by the equity markets. Investors need their money to grow and to outpace inflation so when they need it decades later they aren't receiving less than what they need to keep up with their cost of living. Further, we believe equities are a proven source of potential long-term growth and exposure to them is necessary to beat inflation and achieve growth. Historically, stocks have been the best-performing asset class over ten- and twenty-year periods. However, they are also prone to inevitable, yet unpredictable, periods of large losses and can experience tremendous volatility or price swings along the way, leading to the reasoning behind our second position on the hedge.

Second, we believe market timing to be difficult, if not impossible, to successfully and continuously execute year after year, forever. No one has a crystal ball or knows when the market will top or bottom, regardless of what talking heads say. We believe indicators, fundamental statistics, and other market timing triggers can appear to work for long periods of time before they suddenly don't—this can quickly unwind the many times when they did work. Getting the timing wrong can also cost you either a substantial loss if you exit too late or a substantial gain if you enter too late. For example, after the 2008 Financial Crisis, many investors were unsure when to get back into the stock market. In the first thirty-one days after the market bottomed out, the S&P 500 was up 26.9 percent, an astounding amount over a very short period of time. An investor who participated in the subsequent bull market for the next eight full years would have had a return of 335.7 percent. An investor who arrived fashionably late and missed the first month of that same eight-year period would have had a return of 243.4 percent. While a return of 243.4 percent is certainly impressive, the cost of missing that first month was 92.3 percent. By contrast, the 2000–02 bear market after the dot.com bust took a couple of years to form a bottom, so timing reentry would have been even more difficult. So why try to time the market? If you stay invested at all times, you can reap the rewards more consistently.

Further, we believe attempting to pick specific stocks or sectors is more difficult to successfully execute continuously, year after year. Doing so requires you to successfully and repeatedly time the market, as well as handle the ongoing challenge of knowing which stocks or sectors to buy or sell. Studies show that after adjusting for fees most active managers trail their stated benchmark. Simple probability analysis indicates that some active managers will outperform a passive benchmark and a handful will likely be able to string together multiple periods of outperformance. However, can they repeat their success decade after decade, through good markets and bad? Evidence suggests that it takes luck to consistently pick these outperforming managers (and even if you did, their success can quickly disappear). This is another argument for passive index investing. Thus, the DRS utilizes low-cost, passively managed ETFs to gain its market exposure.

## 2. Hedge Component

Swan's equity buy-and-hold process described in the previous section is not groundbreaking in the least. Many investors implement a passively managed buy-and-hold strategy. Market behemoths like Vanguard and Black-Rock were built around such principles. However, the fatal flaw of passive buy-and-hold strategies is that they don't play defense. If and when markets go down, a passive strategy will fall in lock step with the market.

This is where Swan's DRS has something unique to offer: Our core belief is that the downside risk of major market sell-offs is too great for most investors to bear, so it makes sense to mitigate as much of that risk as possible. Throughout this book we have repeatedly discussed how losses of 20 percent, 30 percent, 40 percent, or more can cripple an investor and destroy even the best-laid plans. That is the *why* behind hedging; the following is a breakdown of the hedge and its benefits.

### • Long-Term Put: LEAP

The DRS hedges by purchasing a long-term put option, or long-term equity anticipation security (LEAP), to protect the equity position against major sell-offs. Put options lock in a sales price for an asset at expiration, should that asset fall in value. The hedge is always in place because we don't profess to know when markets might take a downturn. Just as a homeowner should always maintain fire insurance on a house, the DRS always maintains protection on its equity position. The DRS does not follow a risk-on/risk-off approach where protection may not be in place. We are always hedged.

The price of put options is determined by the market's perception of risk. The DRS buys put options "at the money" or "near the money." This means the strike price for the option is very close to the current market price of the asset. For example, if the S&P 500 has a price level of 2,000, the put option strike price will also be around 2,000. If the S&P 500's price level drops to any level below 2,000, the put will be "in the money," or the put option contract itself is more valuable than the price paid for the contract.

Other strategies might hedge using "out of the money" put options. In the previous example, this might mean the hedge strike price is at, say, 1,700 rather than 2,000. The apparent advantage of this hedge strategy is that put options are cheaper when purchased out-of-the-money, but the major disadvantage is that the investor has more downside risk.

Using an insurance analogy, hedging with out-of-the-money put options is like purchasing a low-premium/high-deductible health insurance plan. Moving the hedge strike lower is analogous to taking on a bigger deductible before protection really kicks in. In the previous example, the market could drop three hundred points and the put option would have little protection until the market declines below the put's strike. Furthermore, if the strategy holds these options to expiration, the options provide zero protection until the market declines below the strike price. Sure, on a month-to-month basis, the cost of protection (premium) might be lower. But if the policy-holder has health problems, they will have to pay much more in out-of-pocket costs before reaching their deductible limits. The DRS was built around the idea of protecting against losses at the outset, not waiting for a steep correction before help arrives.

A disadvantage of hedging with at-the-money put options is their apparent higher up-front cost. However, Swan utilizes cost-minimization techniques when hedging to help mitigate the carrying cost of maintaining the hedge. These techniques are one of the reasons why the DRS uses long-term hedges rather than short-term ones.

Options have a finite lifespan and are effective for weeks, months, or years. But once they expire, they are gone. Thus, the value of the option decreases as it approaches expiration. What is important to note is that the rate at which the option decreases in value is not linear but exponential, decreasing faster as it gets closer to expiration.

The DRS seeks to exploit this time-decay dynamic in its active manage-ment of the hedge. If a significant portion of its contract term passes with substantial value left in the option contract, the DRS "rolls the hedge." This means the DRS sells the existing put option for its market price (based on volatility, moneyness,[1] and time left to expiration) and re-hedges by buying a new long-term put option for a longer time horizon. Unlike many other hedged equity competitors, the DRS does not hold its put options all the way to expiration. These options are traded on a deep and liquid exchange. The DRS remains always hedged, per our philosophy, so that we are not exposed to the steep drop-off in price that happens in the back half of an option's life, nor are we under duress to seek protection in times of market stress when that protection becomes expensive or even cost-prohibitive. So, while the DRS is passively invested in the market, the hedging component is always actively managed.

### • Value of the Re-hedge: Capitalizing on Market Turmoil

Many may view a portfolio hedge as cost, which assumes a short-term view of hedging. We take a longer view. Over a full market cycle, the long-term put option hedge can be a valuable portfolio asset. In times of market stress like a bear or decline, the hedge can provide investors with extra cash to buy more shares—usually when they don't have any extra cash or discipline to do so. As mentioned in the previous section, DRS put options are purchased near the money or at the money. If the price of the index declines, the put option goes in the money and its value goes up.

However, owning a put option does not mean a dollar-for-dollar off-set from the outset. While the equity and hedge portions tend to move in opposite directions, other factors can impact the value of an option. These include things like volatility and time to expiration, which both factor in the price of the option. These additional factors also affect the amount of protection, acting like a deductible on an insurance policy. This deductible is met once the option has gone somewhere in the ballpark of 20-plus percent in the money from its strike. Only after that point will the option cover equity losses on a dollar-for-dollar basis. The DRS approach of using long-term at the money options and rolling those options yearly establishes an annual deductible in the range of 7 percent to 10 percent. This deductible assumes a full year of time decay. If a sell-off happens much earlier in the year, this deductible may be significantly lower.

To continue with an earlier example, assume the S&P 500 had a price level of 2,000 and a put option with a strike price of 2,000 was purchased as a hedge. If the S&P 500 drops 20 percent to a level of 1,600, the holder of the put option can sell based off the 2,000-level strike less the time-value deductible even though the underlying asset is at 1,600. Thus, the DRS put option can become gold during a major market sell-off.

The DRS was built to capitalize on this kind of market turmoil. The idea is similar to the conventional practice of portfolio rebalancing. The DRS typically starts the year with roughly 90 percent of its assets in the market and roughly 10 percent in the hedge. Should the market sell off by 20 percent or more, that ratio will change. As the value of the equity portion sinks, the value of the put option increases. Following a market sell-off, the ratio might look like the chart below, with roughly 70 percent of the assets in the equity and 30 percent in the hedge.

## Figure 8.1. Theoretical Portfolio Ratings

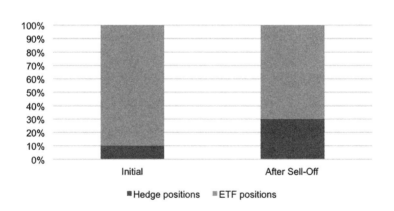

*Source: Swan Global Investments. Hypothetical illustration.*

If the sell-off scenario unfolds as described, the DRS has two options. The DRS could wait around for the market to recover, in which case the equity-to-hedge ratio might eventually rebalance to 90-10, but that represents a huge lost opportunity. In a serious decline, the hedge explodes in value, minimizing losses in the portfolio. Why not capitalize on that gain by selling the now-very valuable hedge for a profit?

In fact, that is exactly what the DRS does. Should the market sell off by a large margin, the DRS will liquidate the existing hedge at a healthy gain (i.e., sell high). A new hedge is purchased, at the money or near the money, to protect the equity at the now-lower market level. The DRS will then take the profits from the sale of the old valuable hedge (less the cost of the new hedge) and buy more shares of the underlying equity that is now priced much lower (i.e., buy low). If and when markets do rebound, the DRS would have bought more equity on the cheap, giving investors more equity shares with a lower average price from which to enjoy the rebound, which may provide more total growth and appreciation over time.

By design, the DRS is a buy low, sell high strategy that generates cash within the portfolio to buy equity at a low price. While other strategies are scrambling to protect against further losses and lick their wounds, the DRS is able to buy the market. This extremely powerful feature allows investors to view sell-offs in a different light, reduce emotional reactions to major market sell-offs, and anticipate the potential buying opportunity.

Of course, there is a risk that the markets will continue to go down following a re-hedge. Such was the case in October 2008 when the DRS sold its extremely profitable hedge and acquired significant additional shares with the market down about 25 percent. The market continued to sell off through the end of the year, and the DRS ended down 4.5 percent after fees versus the S&P 500's loss of 37 percent for the year. Swan doesn't profess to know when the bottom of a market will occur. If we could call the market bottom, obviously we would wait until that precise moment to do the re-hedge. Absent a crystal ball, we rely upon our rules to indicate when we should initiate a re-hedge. In any case, even without timing the bottom, the DRS delivered significant protection and acquired additional shares in 2008 that contributed to helping nearly match the market's gains in 2009.

We believe this re-hedging process to be one of the most attractive features of the DRS. Too often investors tend to get spooked in the face of a major market sell-off and do the worst thing at the worst time. Many panic and sell their investments, and very few see a sell-off as an opportunity to buy at a low point.

The DRS puts the investor in a much more comfortable position to weather storms. The hedge protects them on the downside, so they are likely exposed to fewer losses in a market rout. Moreover, they are sitting on an asset—the put option—that has appreciated in value when everything else is falling. The DRS will systematically take profits from the hedge and put them back to work in the equity markets while remaining fully hedged.

Warren Buffett has said, "Be fearful when others are greedy and be greedy when others are fearful." The DRS allows investors to do exactly that.

### • Carrying the Cost of the Hedge

Someone might ask, "Why always carry the hedge? Why don't you just purchase it right before the market crashes?" Such a thought is easily spoken but near impossible to implement. It goes against our belief that it is difficult, if not impossible, to time the market, especially consistently. We never know when the markets might crash, so we always maintain protection.

Short-term options can be great for short-term risk, such as navigating through an election, an international political event, or the US fiscal cliff (December 2012 to January 2013) or credit downgrade (August 2011). This is assuming one can forecast and properly time the beginning, duration, and aftermath of such short-term events. Overall, longer-term options are much better suited to provide the protection needed in a buy-and-hold strategy through inevitable, yet unpredictable bear markets and crises.

Other strategies out there seek to hedge but do so using put options with an expiration of one, three, or perhaps six months. But hedging with short-dated options is much less effective than using long-term options. It can also be costlier.

The type of major bear markets that the DRS seeks to protect against tends to last a long time, sometimes for years. If a portfolio has protection with, say, a sixty-day put option and the markets crash, investors would have likely benefited as that particular put option goes in the money. But then what? What happens on day sixty-one? Or day seventy-five? Or day ninety? If the markets are still dropping, put options become very expensive as everyone scrambles to protect their assets. If markets are in free fall, it may simply become too expensive to hedge the portfolio. Ironically, a strategy using short-term put option protection might not be able to hedge the portfolio when it needs it the most.

The analogy we like to use at Swan is that hedging in the midst of a crisis is like trying to purchase fire insurance on your house while it is burning down. If you don't have the proper protection already in place, then it is too late. Because the DRS always has hedge protection in place, we are never forced to hedge under duress. This is another key feature that we believe sets our strategy apart.

Using long-term put options that we roll before expiration provides another important feature to DRS investors: protection from any market level. Competitor strategies that allow their options to expire effectively have zero protection unless the market is below their strike price at the time of expiration. Always having a non-zero time value in an asset that you hold long is especially important in a scenario where the market moves up from the initial strike price and then gives back some of those gains.

In the case of a short-term option that expires worthless, 100 percent of the premium paid for the hedge is lost. In the case of a longer-term hedge that is traded well before expiration, the hedge will increase in value when the market declines from any level. Thus, regardless of market gains above the hedge strike, the hedge will provide some cushion from any level. That cushion increases as the market declines because the DRS provides more and more protection the worse it gets, and as noted before, it is never under any duress to purchase a new hedge to protect in the midst of a crisis.

- **Sacrifice a Little Upside to Avoid the Bigger Downside: A Winning Approach**

In up markets the hedge will act as a drag on performance for two reasons. First, the DRS does not have full exposure to the market—roughly 10 percent of the portfolio holdings are in the hedge; the DRS won't see full up-market participation. Second, if the market is up significantly and moves away from the put option's strike price, the put option loses more of its value over the course of the year.

Again, the example of insurance serves us well. If you didn't have to pay for health, homeowners, or auto insurance, you would have a lot more money to spend out of every paycheck. But without insurance, you are fully exposed to downside risk, so sacrificing a bit on the upside is worth the peace of mind on the downside.

## • Protect Gains

There is another key advantage to rolling the hedge on the upside. Every time the DRS rolls the hedge, we set the strike price at or near current market levels. Since the market bottomed out in March 2009, it has risen to successively higher levels for each subsequent year.

By setting the hedge at higher and higher points, the DRS essentially locks in a type of floor at higher levels of the market. Losses from those points have some protection according to our 7 percent to 10 percent defined risk deductible. The ability to lock in annual gains in the market stands in stark contrast to a traditional strategy that can only protect gains in a very inefficient manner by selling a portion of the assets. This typical strategy is inefficient for two reasons. First, the manager would have to sell at a high or risk missing out on the next up move, and second, selling would most likely trigger a taxable event. The DRS approach allows investors to buy and hold core assets and lock in gains with little to no timing risk.

In addition, the DRS is tax efficient. Not only does it avoid realizing capital gains on equity, it can generate and carry forward any capital losses from the hedge. So even if the market is moving up, there are advantages to carrying the hedge.

## • 10 Is Greater than 40

The equity position is protected by a long-term put option, representing roughly 10 percent of the portfolio. This investment is not a sunk cost. The roughly 10 percent is an annual allocation to an inversely correlated security with value that rises and falls in the opposite direction of the underlying asset. That's our 10 percent for portfolio protection, which, by the way, also offers the re-hedge benefits described above.

The traditional and popular 60/40 portfolio construction puts 40 percent of the portfolio into an asset class (bonds) that was meant to serve two functions: portfolio protection and income. With yields on the 10-year US Treasury bonds yielding between 2 percent and 3 percent, there isn't much income to speak of. In fact, with inflation around 2 percent to 3 percent, there isn't any real income from the safest of bond investments. Yet the amount of investment in bonds globally remains high despite low yields. So this must mean the 40 percent is being maintained more for the protection role it may serve. That leaves the remaining 60 percent to drive the vast majority of portfolio return and growth.

The DRS uses only 10 percent for protection, leaving a much larger allocation (90 percent) of the portfolio for equities. Remember, equities have historically been a stronger performing asset class than bonds in terms of total return. Going forward, given either a protracted period of low yields or an eventual rise in yields (which means a loss in bond values), bonds will likely not replicate the returns they have produced over the past nearly four decades. Bill Gross, the famous bond investor and cofounder of Pacific Investment Management Company, discussed the current bull market in bonds and the future of the bond market in his first quarter 2016 outlook, saying, "For over 40 years, asset returns and alpha generation from penthouse investment managers have been materially aided by declines in interest rates, trade globalization and an enormous expansion of credit–that is debt."[2] Gross went on to describe the bond market performance as "remarkable," adding that it "cannot be repeated . . . [Bond yields] would have to drop to -17%" in order to repeat the 7.5% gain over the past 40 years.

In addition, as I've stated before, historical assumptions regarding correlations between bonds and stocks underpinning Modern Portfolio Theory—that they often move in opposite directions—largely broke down in 2008. So bonds may not provide the degree of protection assumed, as they may not be as non-correlated to equities in the next bear market or economic crisis.

As such, we think our 10 percent put option is of greater value to investors over the long term than the 40 percent allocated by many to bonds.

## Managing the Hedge Cost

A flat market is especially revealing when comparing actual costs of the DRS long-term versus other short-term hedging methods. To fully hedge a portfolio using short-term (e.g., weekly, monthly, or quarterly) at the money options may require allocating approximately 2 percent of the portfolio to the hedge for a quarter of the year. In contrast, the DRS long-term options require an allocation of approximately 10 percent.

While this disparity may appear to favor the short-term options, the annual carry cost of the short-term options is far greater. Specifically, in a flat market the short-term options will expire worthless four times per year creating an annual carry cost of potentially up to 8 percent. In the case of the DRS long-term options, we expect a decay of approximately 3 percent to 4 percent for the entire year. By taking advantage of the exponential nature of time decay on an option, Swan has reduced its annual costs for the hedge by approximately 50 percent.

This hedge position is specifically designed to limit a portfolio's exposure to falling markets. The hedge is implemented in a manner that seeks to minimize the out-of-pocket costs of maintaining put option protection, as well as to be a potential profit source for the DRS in times of major market sell-offs. But protection is not free, which leads to the reasoning behind the third part of the strategy, market-neutral option trades.

### 3. Premium-Seeking Option Trades

The DRS could have been designed with only the first two components: a long position in the market and a hedge to protect those holdings. However, in flat or up markets, the carrying cost of the hedge acts as a drag on performance. While we believe it is prudent to always be prepared for a bear market, there is one problem with being always hedged, even though the hedge is managed in a cost-efficient manner—the carrying

cost. Again, protection is not free. To round out the DRS, a third component was added to the mix.

This third component is our short-term option trades. These trades
involve buying and/or selling puts and calls, generally short-term in duration and actively managed. For more on options, please review Appendix 1.
This component seeks not only to help offset the cost of the hedge and provide additional portfolio return, but also to be a source of returns independent from the overall direction of the market. Technically speaking, the goal
of these trades is to collect a small amount of risk premium via the sale of
short-term put options and call options. The risk premium derives from the
relationship between the realized and implied volatility in the market (the
actual and perceived risk by market participant for moves up or down in the
near future), which we explain in detail below. Swan has engaged in various
options strategies, across different market conditions, since 1997, using an
actively managed, transparent, and rules-based approach. We believe

- No options strategy works all the time
- Markets are always evolving
- Thus, *risk* is always evolving
- Therefore, an active approach is necessary

We always look to optimize the risk/reward trade-off of a trade, selecting the appropriate options strategy and defining entry and exit points
based on option market metrics (volatility, skew, term structure) at the time
of trade initiation.

The option trades are designed to be market neutral, meaning that Swan
doesn't care if the market goes up or down in order for the trades to work,
as the trades do not assume a market direction or need to time the market.
Actually, our preference with respect to this particular investment process
step is that, in the short term, the market remains relatively flat, because
that's when premium collection trades are most profitable.

- **How Option Trades Work**

Every option trade has two sides. The buyer of the call (or put) has the right to buy (or sell) a specified asset at a specified price within a certain time frame. For this right, the buyer of the option pays an up-front premium to the writer (seller) of the option. If that right is not exercised within the time frame, the option contract expires as worthless.

To understand the role and motivation of the other side of the trade, let's flip the equation. The writer of the option has the obligation to make up the difference between the strike price and the market price, should the option go in the money. The writer of the option, be it a call or a put, collects a premium for undertaking this risk. But what happens if the option doesn't go in the money? What if, at expiration, the strike price hasn't been breached? Well, count that as a win for the writer of the option. They pocket that premium collected at the sale of the option contract and no longer have an obligation to anyone. Remember that the writer of a put option is hoping the market doesn't go down and the writer of the call option is hoping the market doesn't go up between now and the option's expiration. It is this basic dynamic that the DRS uses with its premium collection-seeking option trades. Unlike the first two components of the strategy, which are very long term in nature, these option trades are short term.

We will never profit by 100 percent of the premium sold; our profit goals for any individual trade are modest. This approach reduces pressure on any individual trade to deliver a significant amount of our annual targets. In addition, it minimizes the risk of any individual trade when the markets move near our preset exit points (i.e., strike price of put and call options).

Historically, this third component of the DRS has been a very valuable and profitable part of our overall solution and is where we spend the majority of our day-to-day efforts. We regard our management of option trades to be a source of "alpha" or "edge" in our overall process.

### • Why Premium-Seeking Option Trades Work

At this point, some people can get confused about the DRS option positions. On one hand, the DRS owns a put option as a hedge. On the other
hand, the DRS sells puts and calls to generate a return. How does one
square that circle?

The difference, and the reason why it works, has to do with the different time horizons of the positions. Both the equity position and the hedge
position are designed to be long-term holdings. The equity is an indefinite
buy-and-hold position designed to participate in bull markets. The hedge is
a long-term put option, the advantages of which we have discussed.

The option trades, however, typically extend out only for a month or
two. The time decay of an option also applies to these short-term options—
they lose value very quickly. However, because the DRS has taken a short
position or sold these options, the fact that they lose value quickly works
in our favor. The trade is designed to work as follows: 1) We collect the
premium initially, 2) the value of the options we sold falls off as they near
expiration, and 3) we are able to then shut down the trade by buying the
options back at a lower price. Repeat.

The reason why we believe this to be a sustainable strategy has to do
with the risk premium frequently displayed between implied and realized
volatility in the markets.

In the market, there is implied volatility, or what the market "thinks"
might happen, and realized volatility, the actual volatility that manifested.
There is usually a gap between these two. Sometimes people will think
volatility will be high but are then met with lower levels of volatility. This
gap between implied and realized volatility can be a source of profit if one
systematically sells overpriced options and collects the premium, and then
buys them back at a lower price at a later date.

More often than not, markets tend to overestimate the amount of volatility present and, as a result, overpay for short-term protection. Of course,
these short-term option trades won't always be profitable for Swan. There
are times when the margin between implied and realized volatility is small,
limiting the theoretical profitability of the trade. Worse, there are times
when the relationship inverts and the realized volatility is higher than the
implied volatility, in which case a volatility harvesting strategy will most

likely be challenged and could be unprofitable. But, more often than not, volatility is overpriced and can be exploited for profit.

Since we believe protection is of paramount importance, we look to find the most cost-effective way to hedge a portfolio (long-term put options), manage the cost of that hedge (rolling the hedge annually), and then use shorter-term option trades each month to help pay for the cost of the long-term protection. This is akin to a car rental company that buys normal car insurance for its fleet, then turns around and sells much more expensive short-term insurance to day-to-day renters. Car insurance websites estimate the average American's monthly cost for coverage is around $150. The daily cost for car rental insurance ranges between $20 and $40 per day, which translates to $600 to $1,200 per month. Why? There is a premium paid for short-term insurance since it is constantly and immediately needed and because those renting the car want to avoid short-term risks. This allows car rental agencies to make their insurance issuance a large source of profit.

## DRS: A Rules-Based, Repeatable Process

Because the DRS is not a tactical strategy that uses timing, stock/sector selection, or leverage to generate its returns, it never has to make decisions on whether to be long or to short the market.

The DRS purchases an asset to gain exposure to a particular market and simultaneously purchases a long-term option to hedge much of the downside risk on a cost-effective and continual basis. The DRS then regularly sells shorter-term, market-neutral options to generate additional return to mitigate the cost of the hedge in a flat or upward-moving market.

This is all a rules-based process. Traders will act and adjust the portfolio as the rules dictate; the DRS is not a "set it and forget it" approach where positions are left unmanaged. Swan does not tactically use options to hedge, meaning we do not arbitrarily decide when or how much to hedge. Rather, the DRS is always invested and always hedged regardless of our view of market conditions. Investors in the DRS do not rely on a crystal ball, but a repeatable, transparent, and scalable process to protect during major declines, provide cash to buy market lows, and provide significant upside exposure to market rallies in a very tax-efficient manner.

Given the rules-based framework, our strategy is truly asset-agnostic, provided there is ample liquidity in the asset class and the underlying or highly correlated options market. As such, the Defined Risk Strategy can be, and has been, applied to various asset classes, including US large-cap (S&P 500), US small-cap (Russell 2000), foreign developed equities (EAFE index), emerging market equities (EM index), real estate investment trusts, gold, and fixed income (TLT index). Swan continues to innovate to deliver investors a better way to invest long term.

9

# DELIVERING THE GOODS– PERFORMANCE REVIEW

"It is no use saying 'we are doing our best.' You have to succeed
in doing what is necessary."
—WINSTON CHURCHILL

I began the Defined Risk Strategy (DRS) in 1997. Since then it has performed through a multitude of crises:

1998—Russian default; Long-Term Capital Management crisis

1999—Dot.com mania and day trading lead to frenzied valuations

2000—Dot.com bubble bursts

2001—9/11 attacks; invasion of Afghanistan

2002—Sarbanes-Oxley Act after accounting scandals at Enron, Tyco,
MCI WorldCom, etc.

2003—The Iraq War initiated

Mid-2000s—Housing bubble inflates

2007–2009—Housing bubble bursts; biggest financial crisis since the
Great Depression

2008—Oil hits $147 per barrel

2009–2012—Euro crisis; period of ultra-loose monetary policy, low rates, and quantitative easing

2010—"Flash Crash" in May; intra-day losses on the Dow Jones Industrial Average are almost 1,000 points

2011—Downgrade of US Treasury debt from AAA to AA

2015–2016—Steep sell-offs based on fears of a hard landing in China

2016—Oil falls to below $30 per barrel as shale-based fracking revolutionizes energy markets; Brexit, election of Donald Trump, and other populist-fueled political developments

2017—US equity markets continue to set all-time highs

Just about every market environment imaginable has happened over the last twenty years:

- The two largest bear markets since World War II
- The second-longest (and still ongoing) bull market in US history
- Losses of more than 50 percent as well as gains of 300-plus percent
- Short-term shocks and corrections
- Two wars and an attack on American soil
- A reversal in the multilateral, collaborative, post-World War II order
- Technological innovations unimaginable in 1997
- Commodities at historic highs as well as lows

For more than twenty years, the DRS has acted the way I expected it would when I devised it. Since its inception, the DRS has outperformed both the S&P 500 and a blended 60/40 stock/bond mix, on both an absolute and risk-adjusted basis, as shown in Figure 9.1. The top line representing the value of $536,540 is the DRS Select Composite, the middle line with the value of $455,551 is the S&P 500 Index, and the last line with the $396,808 value is the 60/40 mix. It's important to keep in mind what that $536,540 line incorporates. It's not just about twenty-plus years. It's all of those crises listed above. The DRS has been battle-tested through all of the aforementioned events and has remained consistent in its investment process and its long-term investment results.

──────  **Figure 9.1. Swan Defined Risk Strategy Select Composite Net of Fees**  ──────

Growth of $100,00 – July 1, 1997 to December 31, 2018

$504,563
$424,337
$383,648

DRS: $504,563    S&P: $424,337    60/40: $383,648

*Source: Swan Global Investments; Morningstar. Barclays U.S. Aggregate Bond Index and the S&P 500 Index are unmanaged indices and cannot be invested into directly. Past performance is no guarantee of future results. Swan DRS results are from the Select Composite, net of fees, as of 12/31/2018. Structures mentioned may not be available within your broker/dealer.*

## Measuring Success

At this point it is important to discuss how the performance of the DRS might be viewed and how best to measure whether the strategy is delivering the goods. But first, I want to explain some ways investment returns are reported and what investors should know when reviewing performance of this or any other strategy.

In a world of instant updates and in an industry focused on short-term performance, investors often fixate on chasing one-, three-, or five-year returns or beating the market. For investors with long-term goals, the most important question is: Will you achieve that goal on time?

Instead of fixating on short-term returns or focusing on beating the market in such short time frames, we encourage investors to take a longer view and consider looking at different measurements of returns or benchmarks. We believe it's about achieving the desired end results. I began with that purpose in mind and developed the DRS to provide the greatest probability of getting me to my goal over the many market cycles I knew would come.

But how do you look at returns? The most common investment industry method uses trailing returns. Trailing returns, or point-to-point returns, are essentially a snapshot of the past, going back over a chosen period and starting with an anchor date, such as the latest quarter or one-year, three-year, or five-year returns. The problem with trailing returns is that they examine only that specified block of time and may engender recency bias. If an investment or strategy just posted a really good quarter or year, that recent performance shines in the trailing return analysis of that period. However, if you were to move that anchor date and review the same block of time, you might find a very different result. In reality, all people do not begin investing in an asset at the same time. So two investors who made the same exact investment (stock or mutual fund, for example) but initiated it a month or a quarter apart could have very different experiences even though they bought into the same investment. Looking only at a recent trailing return would not reflect this reality.

As noted in Chapter 7, we believe rolling returns offer a more comprehensive view of returns—as well as of a manager's or strategy's effectiveness and comprehensiveness—as these examine a fixed period based on different start dates. Looking at the average three-year rolling return for a given investment can show you the return, or experience, investors would have over any three-year period, even if they began investing on different dates. Through the lens of rolling returns, periods of bad performance or a breakdown in a manager's stock-picking strategy will be revealed. A strategy that has consistent rolling returns over periods from three to twenty years is a strategy with a higher probability of offering investors a more predictable set of future returns. Thus, rolling returns are very revealing.

The side-by-side rolling period chart (Figure 7.6) in Chapter 7 (what we affectionately call the "spaghetti & rope" chart) speaks volumes to the consistency of the DRS to deliver, in this case over ten-year rolling periods, which included both bull and bear markets.

## The Target Return Band—The Right Benchmark

The Defined Risk Strategy is distinct—traditional investment classifications don't fit our strategy, and standard indices are not ideal benchmarks. The usual way people measure a fund's short-term performance does not give an accurate portrayal of the strategy. Beyond long-term rolling returns, the best way to evaluate the consistency and repeatability of the DRS is through the prism of our Target Return Band (TRB).

As stated, the goal of the DRS is to help investors reach their long-term goals. We focus on generating stable returns year after year, while potentially protecting investors' capital over time. Because Swan follows a very systematic approach and much of the DRS's returns depend on whatever the market does, we can estimate with a fair degree of accuracy where our returns might fall in any given year.

The TRB illustrates the three main elements of the strategy, our expectations for the strategy, and how those expectations are met on an annual basis. We devised the TRB because comparing funds' performances to the S&P 500 on a yearly, quarterly, monthly, or even daily basis mirrors the myopic focus many analysts have on individual companies beating quarterly earnings estimates. So how do we give investors assurance that they are on track to meet their investing goals? While we believe in longer-term metrics, we have annual measures to assure us that the strategy is working as it's supposed to. Figure 9.2 shows the TRB graph with our actual performance versus the S&P 500 since 1997.

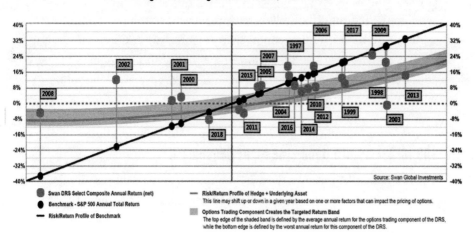

Figure 9.2. Target Return Band, 1997-2018

*Source: Swan Global Investments; Morningstar. The S&P 500 Index is an unmanaged index and cannot be invested into directly. Swan DRS returns are from the Select Composite, net of all fees. Note: This chart is for illustration purposes, not a guarantee of future performance. It should not serve as the sole determining factor for making investment decisions.*

The returns for the DRS Select Composite (a separately managed account launched July 1, 1997) over the past twenty-one years are all mapped on the graph. In any given year, it is our goal that returns of the DRS will be within or above the light gray shaded band area shown in the graph. In nineteen of the twenty-one years, we have achieved that goal. Let's break this down and explain each part. You can see the consistency of returns versus expectations.

## Setting the Benchmark and Risk/Return Profile

Figure 9.3 illustrates the first two components of the DRS: equity plus the hedge.

### Figure 9.3. Target Return Band: Equity and Hedge

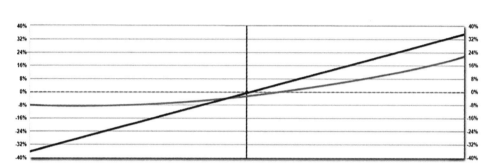

*Source: Swan Global Investments. This chart is for illustration purposes, not a guarantee of future performance. The charts and graphs contained herein should not serve as the sole determining factor for making investment decisions.*

The diagonal dark line represents the risk/return profile of our passive buy-and-hold equity investment. If the equity market goes up or down, the buy-and-hold position gains or loses dollar-for-dollar with the market. The curved gray line represents the redefined risk/return profile created by combining the buy-and-hold equity position with our hedge, a long-term put option (long-term equity anticipation security, or LEAP). The curved line lags the market on the upside (right side of the chart), but still slopes upward, meaning the hedged equity captures upside continually. In down markets (left side of chart), the curved line flattens out as the market continues to drop. So in any given year, the return is calculated by combining the first two components of the DRS (equity plus hedge). Look at the chart and identify a given annual return for the underlying equity market. By looking at the curved line, you can then determine the corresponding hedged equity return. That is the essence of defined risk, and the main value proposition of our Defined Risk Strategy. You can participate and grow wealth by investing in the equity markets, but define your risk of loss on an annual basis.

## Creating the Targeted Return

In the graph below we incorporate the impact layering the premium-seeking option trades on the hedged equity risk/return profile.

——————— **Figure 9.4. Target Return Band: Equity, Hedge, Option Trades** ———————

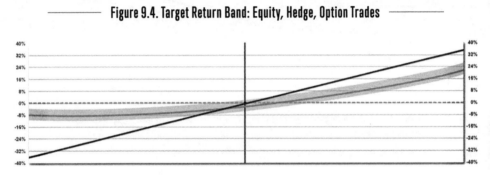

*Source: Swan Global Investments. This chart is for illustration purposes, not a guarantee of future performance. The charts and graphs contained herein should not serve as the sole determining factor for making investment decisions.*

The light gray shaded region around the curved line is the anticipated effect of overlaying Swan's short-term premium collection trades on the hedged-equity position. We expect that returns of the DRS will be within or above the light gray shaded area (although, of course, at times it may not). Figure 9.4 shows how our strategy should perform overall in each year, depending on various outcomes in the market. For example, if the market returns 20 percent, then we would expect to return between 6 percent and 15 percent. Conversely, if the market loses 20 percent, then we would expect a loss of between -5 percent and -14 percent.

Of course, there is no guarantee that returns will be generated at the same average as the historical average going back to the DRS's inception in July 1997. Past performance is no guarantee of future results. (Remember, that's one of the great flaws of MPT.) Averages mask numbers above and below them and change over time. Premium-seeking option trading component returns can vary greatly and can lose money. However, in our experience, most of the time the markets reward short-term systematic option sellers due to the volatility risk premia discussed in the previous chapter. We believe our active management of option trades improves on the passive collection of risk premia (i.e., the gap between implied and realized volatility) and increases the probability that we will capture the maximum amount of risk premia given a specific set of market conditions.

Essentially, the TRB serves as the best way to measure, or benchmark, our results over time. Defining risk in the way we have makes building a financial plan or portfolio model easier as you have a more predictable spectrum of returns.

## The DRS: A Multi-Asset Approach

Thus far, we have focused the discussion on our Select Composite with our S&P 500 strategy; however, we have also seen the DRS work in the same way when applied to other asset classes. The DRS "engine" can be placed into different car models. The past few years, we rolled out the strategy in asset classes for emerging markets, foreign developed markets, small-cap markets, and more. Figure 9.5 shows the TRB with real returns of the DRS when applied to the main categories of equities, since their inception, and their corresponding indexes: US large-cap equities (S&P 500), US small-cap equities (Russell 2000), foreign developed equities (EAFE index), and emerging market equities (EM index). You can see how the annual returns of each application of the DRS has, with two exceptions (2003 and 2018-DRS Select [S&P 500]), been on or above the TRB.

## Figure 9.5. Target Return Band: Real DRS Returns, 1997-2018

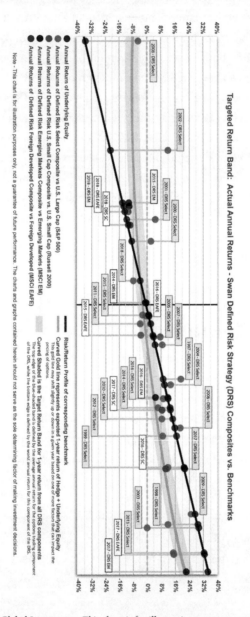

*Source: Swan Global Investments. This chart is for illustration purposes, not a guarantee of future performance. The charts and graphs contained herein should not serve as the sole determining factor for making investment decisions. The results above refer to the DRS Select Composite, the DRS US Small Cap Composite, DRS Emerging Markets Composite, and the DRS Foreign Developed Composite respectively, net of fees.*

The TRB demonstrates the consistency of DRS returns across asset classes and reflects the fact that our investment process is repeatable. The DRS has proven therefore to be asset class neutral; that is, we can generate returns in or above a predictable band of expectations or targeted returns relative to the underlying equity index itself, regardless of the asset class, and thus can aid investors and advisors in building a hedged diversified portfolio. As diversification is important, Swan has endeavored to offer the DRS across other asset classes. Ultimately, we believe a hedged, globally diversified portfolio is better than a globally diversified portfolio over the long term.

## Measuring Portfolio Impact Over Time

Swan uses the TRB as its benchmark every year. Of course, the DRS also is compared against more traditional benchmarks. Figure 9.6 compares the DRS (**line ending with $504,231**) against two common benchmarks, the S&P 500 Total Return Index (**ending with $424,337**) and a composite of 60 percent S&P 500 Index and 40 percent Barclays U.S. Aggregate Bond Index (**ending with $383,648**).

### Figure 9.6. Swan Defined Risk Strategy Select Composite Net of Fees

DRS: $504,563     S&P: $424,337     60/40: $383,648

*Source: Swan Global Investments; Morningstar. Barclays U.S. Aggregate Bond Index and the S&P 500 Index are unmanaged indices and cannot be invested into directly. Past performance is no guarantee of future results. Swan DRS results are from the Select Composite, net of fees, as of 12/31/2018. Structures mentioned may not be available within your broker/dealer.*

As of July 1, 2018, the DRS has done quite well relative to well-known benchmarks, averaging 0.84 percent to 1.55 percent a year better, after fees, than the S&P 500 and 60/40 benchmarks.

It's also worth looking at some of the risk statistics for the DRS over the past twenty-plus years. After all, we claim to help smooth the ride of the S&P 500, while investing nearly 90 percent of our assets in our corresponding version of the DRS in the S&P 500. In terms of volatility, the DRS's standard deviation (volatility of moves up and down) has been about two-thirds of that of the S&P 500, or 9.37 percent versus 14.82 percent. The beta (sensitivity to moves in the S&P 500) of the DRS to the S&P 500 is 0.30, meaning the DRS over time has not been very sensitive to market movements. We typically see our overall return stream as more stable, similar to a balanced fund (hence the 60/40 benchmark). Since the DRS's inception, not only have its average annual returns been much better than those of the 60/40 portfolio, but also the standard deviation is close to the 60/40 and the beta is much lower. Further, the maximum drawdown, or loss, for the DRS in any month since inception is nearly half that of the 60/40 portfolio and one-third that of the S&P 500. So the DRS has provided a higher average annual return while protecting capital better than these two benchmarks, all while delivering a fairly smooth ride.

When we break out the performance of the DRS on a year-by-year basis, we gain even more insight. Figure 9.7 shows the returns for the DRS and the S&P 500 and 60/40 benchmarks since 1997. As expected, the DRS typically trails the S&P 500 in the years when the markets are up. However, the advantage of hedging downside risk is quite evident in the five years that the markets were down. There, the protective power of the hedge is quite evident.

## Figure 9.7. Swan DRS Select Composite vs. S&P 500 Index vs. 60/40

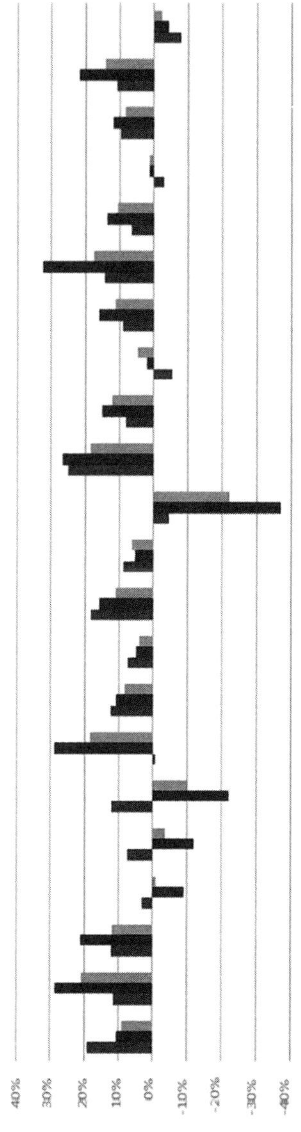


| | 1997 | 1998 | 1999 | 2000 | 2001 | 2002 | 2003 | 2004 | 2005 | 2006 | 2007 | 2008 | 2009 | 2010 | 2011 | 2012 | 2013 | 2014 | 2015 | 2016 | 2017 | 2018 |
|---|---|---|---|---|---|---|---|---|---|---|---|---|---|---|---|---|---|---|---|---|---|---|
| Swan DRS | 19.17% | 11.55% | 12.26% | 3.17% | 7.46% | 12.22% | -0.65% | 12.28% | 7.47% | 18.14% | 8.81% | -4.50% | 25.00% | 8.10% | -5.38% | 9.01% | 14.34% | 6.52% | -2.93% | 9.59% | 10.83% | -7.40% |
| S&P 500 | 10.58% | 28.58% | 21.04% | -9.10% | -11.89% | -22.10% | 28.68% | 10.88% | 4.91% | 15.79% | 5.49% | -37.00% | 26.46% | 15.06% | 2.11% | 16.00% | 32.39% | 13.69% | 1.38% | 11.96% | 21.83% | -4.38% |
| 60/40 | 9.01% | 20.98% | 12.00% | -0.99% | -3.71% | -9.82% | 18.48% | 8.30% | 4.00% | 11.12% | 6.22% | -22.06% | 18.40% | 12.13% | 4.69% | 11.31% | 17.56% | 10.62% | 1.28% | 8.31% | 14.21% | -2.35% |

*Source: Swan Global Investments; Morningstar. Barclays U.S. Aggregate Bond Index and the S&P 500 Index are unmanaged indices and cannot be invested into directly. Past performance is no guarantee of future results. Swan DRS results are from the Select Composite, net of fees, as of 12/31/2018. Structures mentioned may not be available within your broker/dealer.*

# Pain Index: Measuring Loss in Dollars

The DRS was built by an investor, for investors. I hated losing money then, and rest assured, I still do. I understand what behavioral finance research tells us: Investors care much more about big losses than big wins, and losses affect our psychology more than wins. The industry, which is still largely guided by MPT, says investors are risk averse and therefore it measures risk as volatility. Investor surveys and behavioral research repeatedly demonstrate that investors are actually loss averse, and therefore, drawdown (a measure of absolute loss) is a more appropriate measure of risk. The pain index, appropriately named, does just that and more.

Standard deviation, the common industry metric for measuring volatility, measures the volatility of individual returns around a mean return. Unfortunately, standard deviation makes no distinction between the "good" observations that fall above the mean and the "bad" returns that fall below the mean. Most investors would not punish a manager with a high standard deviation if a good portion of the volatility was upside volatility. Standard deviation doesn't account for the timing of negative returns, either. If, for example, a decade has half a dozen exceptionally bad months, standard deviation cannot tell whether these bad observations were randomly scattered throughout the decade or if they were all concentrated within a narrow time frame.

Most important, most investors don't think of risk in terms of standard deviation; they view it in terms of capital preservation. Standard deviation is a classroom concept; capital preservation is a real-world issue.

The pain index measures the depth, duration, and frequency of losses. It effectively graphs the amount of loss between the break-even line and the investment's drawdown (loss) line. The deeper, longer, and more frequent the losses, the greater the pain. Obviously, an investor would prefer that volume to be as small as possible—the smaller the pain index, the better. Zero would be best, indicating the manager never lost money. The following drawdown graph (Figure 9.8) is an example of what this metric looks like and better illustrates the impact of devastating bear markets.

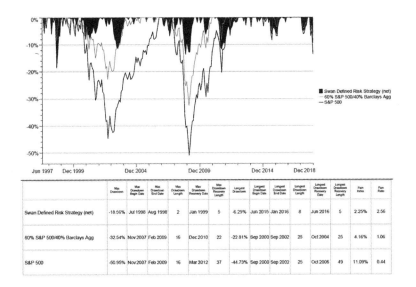

Figure 9.8. Drawdown, July 1997-December 2018

| | Max Drawdown | Max Drawdown Begin Date | Max Drawdown End Date | Max Drawdown Length | Max Drawdown Recovery Date | Max Drawdown Recovery Length | Longest Drawdown | Longest Drawdown Begin Date | Longest Drawdown End Date | Longest Drawdown Length | Longest Drawdown Recovery Date | Longest Drawdown Recovery Length | Pain Index | Pain Ratio |
|---|---|---|---|---|---|---|---|---|---|---|---|---|---|---|
| Swan Defined Risk Strategy (net) | -18.56% | Jul 1998 | Aug 1998 | 2 | Jan 1999 | 5 | -6.29% | Jun 2015 | Jan 2016 | 8 | Jun 2016 | 5 | 2.25% | 2.56 |
| 60% S&P 500/40% Barclays Agg | -32.54% | Nov 2007 | Feb 2009 | 16 | Dec 2010 | 22 | -22.81% | Sep 2000 | Sep 2002 | 25 | Oct 2004 | 25 | 4.16% | 1.06 |
| S&P 500 | -50.95% | Nov 2007 | Feb 2009 | 16 | Mar 2012 | 37 | -44.73% | Sep 2000 | Sep 2002 | 25 | Oct 2005 | 49 | 11.09% | 0.44 |

*Source: Zephyr StyleADVISOR. Barclays U.S. Aggregate Bond Index and the S&P 500 Index are unmanaged indices and cannot be invested into directly. Past performance is no guarantee of future results. Swan DRS results are from the Select Composite, net of fees, as of 12/31/2018.*

The drawdown graph shows the peak-to-trough (highest point to lowest point) losses during two bear markets. Since the start of this millennium, we've seen the two biggest bear markets since World War II. During the dot.com bust, the S&P 500 was down almost 45 percent. In the 2008 Crisis, the S&P 500 lost more than half of its value. Although losses in the dot.com bust were not quite as steep as those inflicted by the 2008 Crisis, the duration of the dot.com bear market was longer. That bear market consisted of three years of losses, and the time it took to recover was even longer. Given the choice of steeper losses or a longer time underwater, many investors would likely prefer neither.

Again, we see how the DRS performed during these two very traumatic markets. Although the DRS is not impervious to losses, they are manageable, thereby allowing for a quicker recovery. Less time spent losing money means more time your money can grow through compounding. This is not an accidental characteristic, but inherent to the DRS's fundamental design. Everything mentioned in the previous chapter about how the DRS is built—hedging against major market sell-offs, capitalizing on profits in the hedge, participating in up markets—is manifested in these numbers and in this graph.

## How the Hedge Impacts Performance

We often hear, "What does portfolio protection cost? Am I not dooming myself to inferior performance if I'm always paying for protection?"

It depends on your time period. As I mentioned in Chapter 7, if you have a short-term investment timeline and therefore a short-term view of hedging, you may generally see hedging as a cost or drag on performance, except of course if a bear market rears its ugly head during your short investment period. We expect that the hedge will create some drag on performance in bull markets and flat markets (assuming a constant volatility) and generate profits in bear markets. The longevity and price appreciation of bull and bear markets will determine whether the hedge provides a net drag or improvement over any particular market cycle. The bigger and longer the advance, the more the cost in terms of less up capture. Conversely, the bigger and longer the sell-off or bear market, the greater the profit. This excerpt was taken from our own research:

> Despite the fact that we expect the DRS to underperform the market in most years when the market rallies, we believe that the DRS can offer competitive returns versus the market over an entire investment cycle . . . The long-term cost of the hedge protection has been relatively low over the implementation period since inception in mid-1997. The performance of just the DRS underlying equity and hedge alone has nearly matched the return performance of the S&P 500 with substantially lower risk, much lower standard deviation, and lower beta (i.e., a smoother ride). The addition of option

premium has only improved the relative performance of the DRS versus the S&P 500.[1]

The long-term cost is ultimately the combination of upside and downside market capture.

## Upside and Downside Market Capture

Investment expert and journalist John Nyaradi explains the importance of protecting assets against downside risk and the effect of that protection on long-term returns: "If you don't lose money during downturns, you only have to capture roughly 30 percent of the upside move of a bull market to beat buy and hold."[2]

Although we have not verified or validated Nyaradi's specific 30 percent claim, it is consistent with our experience and analysis of DRS historical outperformance over a period of more than twenty-one years. We have also done some hypothetical studies, which showed that a portfolio that captures 52 percent in an up quarter and only 16 percent during a down quarter will handily outperform a benchmark that gets 100 percent of each. This, of course, is backed by our actual 52 percent quarterly up capture of the S&P 500 and 16 percent quarterly down capture since our July 1997 inception and our outperformance of the S&P 500 over that time period.

The takeaway is that investors should not solely focus on the upside performance of an asset or asset class, but rather on a return of that asset over an entire market cycle. It is irrelevant what a strategy returns if you lose most of those gains in the next bear market.

## Addressing Underperformance

It is only fair that we take a moment to address two periods of underperformance. As we have always stated, there is no single strategy that will work all the time. Every strategy will have periods of underperformance. Anyone who tells you differently shouldn't be trusted. With that in mind, let's look at the DRS's worst performance in both absolute and relative terms to the market.

## Worst Absolute Returns

In 2018, a year that can be described as a perfect storm of market conditions, the DRS posted the worst annual return in its history. While 2017 had many experts saying low volatility was the new norm, 2018 appeared to be a reaction to the previous year as it introduced volatility in a big way. The S&P 500 finished the year negative at -4.46%, making it the market's first negative year since 2008.

The year may have seemed like a "typical year" for investors, but it had record-breaking corrections and rare occurrences. It was one of the worst years across asset classes in the past decade—there was nowhere to hide. Both domestic and international equities, fixed income, high yield, and even commodities such as gold and oil, finished the year in the red.

The year contained whipsaws and numerous fast, large moves. While this kind of sudden volatility can be detrimental to any investment strategy, it was a very trying environment for the DRS. The three components of the DRS—equal weight, hedge, and option premium trades—were all challenged in 2018.

The first quarter of 2018 started with a historically rapid rise of over 7% followed by a quick 10% correction before rallying and selling off again. This kind of back and forth whipsaw movement and the DRS's reaction resulted in a weak start for the strategy. The equal weight equity component lagged behind the cap weighted S&P 500 market, and the option premium trades were hurt by the short-term volatility spike in January and February. In contrast, the second and third quarters were a smoother ride for investors, and the option premium trades were able to claw back some previous losses by the end of the third quarter.

But what a difference a quarter makes. The S&P 500 ended the third quarter up 10.56% but then dropped -13.52% in the fourth quarter whereas the DRS lost -9.33%. The strategy was able to provide some defense and offset some of the losses of this drawdown. The more the market went down, the more the hedge acted like a brake. However, the market did not fall to the point where the hedge offsets all market losses. It's important to remember that the hedging component of the strategy is most beneficial during large, protracted bear markets: The more the market goes down, the more valuable the hedge becomes.

There was not a single, "smoking gun" that was responsible for 2018's underperformance. Instead it was a combination of several smaller factors in the first and fourth quarters that conspired and led to the worst year in the DRS's history.

## Worst Relative Returns

On a relative basis, 2003 was the worst year in DRS's history, as it lost -0.65 percent compared to the total return of the S&P 500's 28.68 percent on the year. This underperformance came from the hedge component of the DRS. At the end of the three-year bear market from 2000 to 2002, the hedge component was not implemented in a market-neutral fashion—the only time in DRS history. A judgment call was made to over-hedge the portfolio, taking an overly bearish stance versus a market-neutral position. In other words, we positioned the hedge with a downward directional bias, assuming the market would continue to go lower at the end of 2002 and the start of 2003. This bearish stance proved correct at the end of 2002 but a tactical error in 2003. Following the successful conclusion of the first stage of the Iraq War, markets rallied significantly after three years in the doldrums. While the net effect of outperformance in 2002 and underperformance in 2003 was negligible, the negative impact on 2003 in performance and expectations was costly. The put option hedge lost most of its value, causing a significant performance gap between the DRS and the S&P 500 in 2003.

We learned two valuable lessons. First, Swan's core bias against market timing is the correct approach. Second, even with this huge 29 percent underperformance, Swan's ten-year average annualized return was still better than the S&P 500's. This just accentuates the critical importance of preventing downside losses rather than capturing all the upside. Swan is often asked, "What is to prevent us from making a similar decision with an upward or downward bias in the future?" The answer is, "We learned our lesson." It didn't work, and market timing is just not worth the risk. Since then, the DRS has not taken on any directional biases nor will it in the future. It's now part of our codified strategy execution and rules-based process. As we have stated, market timing is difficult and all it takes is one wrong call to experience tremendous variation in performance from the market.

## Expectations and Goals During Bull and Bear Markets

As pleased as we are with the long-term performance of the DRS, an investor should never put money in a strategy based solely on historical performance. Choosing a proper investment strategy should depend more upon its underlying logic and whether or not the investor believes the strategy to be transparent, disciplined, and repeatable. The numbers should only be viewed as an example of possibilities across various market conditions.

To summarize, it is important to have proper expectations during periods of rising markets (bull markets) and falling markets (bear markets).

We expect that the DRS will underperform in bull markets and outperform in bear markets, thanks to several factors, including: (1) size of the move, (2) duration of the move, (3) change in volatility, and (4) profit/loss of option trading component. Generally speaking, the greater the magnitude, speed, and duration of the move up, the greater the chance for DRS underperformance. This could be buffered by any premium from the option-selling component of the DRS. Specifically, the premium component can potentially increase upside capture in up markets, help pay for some or all of the hedge in flat markets, and reduce out-of-pocket losses in a down market. Losses in this third investment process component have the opposite effect but have been limited to only three calendar years of the twenty since the DRS's inception.

Swan's three goals in bull markets are (1) share in as much upside as possible, (2) lock in or hedge those gains by re-hedging the long positions each year (including original investment) in anticipation of the next bear market, and (3) generate as much risk premium as possible.

Swan's three goals in bear markets are (1) minimize downside exposure,

(2) recognize profits from the hedge and reinvest in additional shares using the profits from a re-hedge, and (3) generate as much option risk premium as possible.

The DRS is designed to profit from a bear market or large sell-off by selling an underlying asset's highly profitable put option after it has increased in value, and re-hedging the portfolio at a lower cost and lower strike price put option. The DRS benefits from large magnitude sell-offs due to the re-hedge component, some form of which may play out as I've outlined in Chapter 4. The re-hedge process is designed to substantially lessen the recovery period versus a buy-and-hold approach. Most important, it aims to help investors Sleep Well at Night (SWAN) with consistent, low volatility returns that require no timing or predictive super powers.

## In It for the Long Game

Concern is growing throughout the financial industry about the short-term nature of investors' decisions, holding periods, and time horizons. Markets are too focused on daily and weekly moves and quarterly earnings reports. Investors used to hold securities for years; these days, the average holding period may be months or even weeks. The most egregious example of short-term focus is high-frequency trading where instruments are bought and then sold in fractions of a second. We have always maintained that the proper time frame for measuring success is a full market cycle—a bull market and a bear market. Investors will face many full market cycles during their investing lives, and they never know when those bear markets will come—or if one may appear right before they need their money. So it holds that they should find a way to invest that increases their probability of success over many market cycles. Otherwise, they may get distracted getting in and out of holdings, often with little but fees to show for it, like frantically switching lanes in bumper to bumper traffic.

A full market cycle unfolds over the course of years, not months or days. The DRS is designed to protect against bear markets rather than short-term corrections because bear markets usually last one or more years and take several years to recover. Some investors might argue that bear markets are so infrequent as to make active risk management unnecessary. Obviously, we disagree. The data shared throughout this book illustrates how often bear markets can arrive and how devastating they can be. This current bull market is the second longest in US history, and it would be easy for investors to become complacent. That's just human nature. But, extrapolating historical risk and returns into the future is dangerous to your financial life.

Innovation demands solutions on an absolute and risk-adjusted basis over an entire investment cycle. It also requires a solution that will succeed over a wide range of market conditions since the future is unknown. We will never accept any strategy, including ours, as perfect and without room for improvement. We constantly look for ways to enhance our strategy while maintaining its core principles and fundamental design. We have a responsibility to both improve and maintain the strategy that investors have chosen based on our long-term success. This balance is difficult but crucial in our commitment to our investors.

More and more strategies that focus on risk management have entered the marketplace. Since the 2008 Financial Crisis, the marketplace has been flooded with solutions seeking to generate DRS-like results. Although we are not aware of anyone with a solution quite like ours, there are similar ones. Clearly, investors are interested in downside protection. However, these new strategies in the liquid alternative or options-based space are mostly immature and have not been battle-tested through an actual bear market, much less two. Real-world experience through a crisis is invaluable. We have plenty of comparison writings on our website, and I've listed them in Appendix 2 for those who want to read further on this topic.

The bottom line: We want the hedged equity investment space to proliferate because we believe such strategies provide real and substantial value to investors regardless of the market environment. This is true even if we have to share the space with others. Everyone wins.

We are trying to fundamentally change the way investors think about risk and redefine how to invest (risk management is the key) using the new tools available.

# I0

# TAKING CONTROL

"The world as we have created it is a process of our thinking.
It cannot be changed without changing our thinking."
—ALBERT EINSTEIN

The journey over the last two decades has certainly been an eventful one, and it is far from over. When I set out to create a better investment solution, I had no idea what the future might hold. I did not foresee any of the major events that we have discussed in these pages.

Back in the halcyon days of the mid-1990s I knew trouble was brewing, but I had no idea when or how these problems would manifest themselves. I didn't know when markets might go south or what the impetus would be for a correction. Conversely, I didn't know when a bull market might start or how long it might run. And because of that, I wanted a solution for my money that was prepared no matter what.

The future holds challenges that might make those of the last two decades seem miniscule in comparison. There are plenty to keep us all awake at night. You need to put your assets, and your future, in the highest branch in the tallest tree.

The financial industry is going through a period of dramatic change. The demographics of the country are changing, the regulatory environment is changing, and the solutions offered are changing. After the 2008

Financial Crisis, there was a lot of distrust in Wall Street and the way they do things. There still is.

A massive shift into exchange-traded funds (ETFs) and passive management has been driving disruption across the financial industry. For example, there has been a tenfold increase in available ETFs from 2005 to mid-2017. And according to data compiled by TABB Group, 20 percent to 25 percent of all shares traded on US exchanges today are shares of ETFs.

### Figure 10.1. Global ETF and ETP Growth

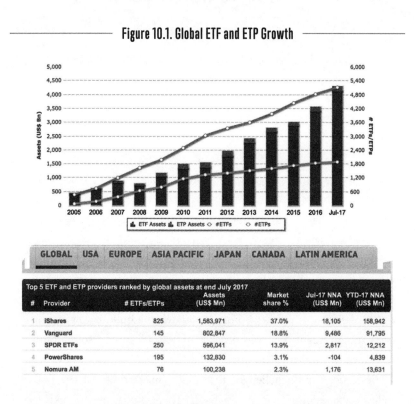

| Top 5 ETF and ETP providers ranked by global assets at end July 2017 | | | | | |
|---|---|---|---|---|---|
| #  Provider | # ETFs/ETPs | Assets (US$ Mn) | Market share % | Jul-17 NNA (US$ Mn) | YTD-17 NNA (US$ Mn) |
| 1  iShares | 825 | 1,583,971 | 37.0% | 18,105 | 158,942 |
| 2  Vanguard | 145 | 802,847 | 18.8% | 9,486 | 91,795 |
| 3  SPDR ETFs | 250 | 596,041 | 13.9% | 2,817 | 12,212 |
| 4  PowerShares | 195 | 132,830 | 3.1% | -104 | 4,839 |
| 5  Nomura AM | 76 | 100,238 | 2.3% | 1,176 | 13,631 |

*Source: ETFGI data sourced from ETF/ETP sponsors, exchanges, regulatory filings, Thomas Reuters/Lipper, Bloomberg, publicly available sources, and data generated in-house.*

The movement from active to passive investment management shows that many investors don't see the point in paying extra fees for professional management that offers the same or similar returns as a passive index fund. Passive assets have grown considerably in the past ten years. As they forget the pain of the last bear market, or respond to the promise of convenience, more and more investors have begun adopting strategies based on Modern Portfolio Theory (MPT), robo-advisors, or other passive buy-and-hold solutions.

The compression of fees, the disintermediation of players, and consumers tiring of the solutions offered also drive demands for change in the industry. Changes are normal aspects of a functioning market and are good for the consumer. The saying that "a good plan today is better than a great plan tomorrow" is very apropos. No one can know exactly where things are headed, but you don't want to be left without a chair when the music stops. You need to anticipate where the market is going, get there first, establish your position, and then bring others along.

Swan Global Investments is well positioned to take advantage of these changes. I believe we will be one of the leading agents for change, especially when it comes to managing downside risk in a portfolio. I believe this so strongly that virtually all of my liquid net worth is invested across our products. I would not have it any other way. Not only should cooks eat their own cooking, but I believe this meal to be the best available to achieve my goals.

## Industry in Need of Redefinition

I had a meeting in 2009 or 2010 with a pension consultant who represented a very large and well-known widget producer. This consultant admitted he was okay with losing 27 percent of the client's portfolio in 2008—which, by the way, is roughly what a 60/40 portfolio returned that year. In his mind, there was no other solution. I've since had many similar meetings. Too many investors, individuals, and institutions alike don't know of any other way. The industry hasn't offered much in the way of real innovation— most portfolios today still represent something akin to the 60/40. "Not-so-Modern Portfolio Theory," the reliance on diversification through asset allocation, is still the foundation of most finance curriculums, professional advisory practices, and even institutional portfolios. Swan will never be okay with losing 27 percent. Would you?

The investment landscape has changed since MPT was first devised and the 60/40 portfolio (or some close derivation thereof) became the dominant portfolio model. In launching my investment strategy, I sought to redefine the risk/return profile of long-term equity investing because the world changes and natural law dictates we change with it. Over the years, my company has sought to redefine how investors invest. It's about taking control of risk to the degree you can to provide the greatest chance of long-term success in the widest range of possible environments. I hope I have sparked your desire to take control of your investments and financial future, while you can.

## Taking Control

With the reverse of quantitative easing, the low interest rate environment, changing demographics, ballooning costs of entitlements, and the ever-present geopolitical risk, there are a lot of uncontrollable threats. But I believe we, as investors, can do something to protect our financial well-being and our future goals. While no investment company can solve these problems, we can at least provide investors with a strategy that is logical, proven, transparent, and repeatable. We cannot avoid market turmoil entirely, but we can manage and control the risks. I have outlined what I do and what I offer, but there are others who are joining in the space as well. Whether you decide to go with us or go with another strategy, there are some important elements to consider:

- What does the strategy offer me?
- Has it been tested? If so, has it been tested in many different environments?
- How transparent is it?
- Is the process repeatable and the returns consistent?

The Defined Risk Strategy (DRS) emerged from a desire for an investment approach that could allow someone to benefit from the equities market while reducing the risks inherent in equities investing. The DRS was designed to avoid the inherent vulnerabilities in passive asset allocation investment strategies and the difficulties in selecting individual stocks for investment and timing the overall market, and to protect against market risk. Even a well-diversified portfolio can be hurt when all of the components decline at the same time. Plus short-term emotional decisions or reactions to large market declines can wreck even the best-laid financial plans. As such, we believe a hedged diversified global portfolio will better serve the interests of long-term investors than a diversified global portfolio.

If we have a better understanding of history, of natural law, and of modern culture, then we also understand that decisions we make about our government and our personal values are not made in the abstract or separated from our financial security—indeed, they are part and parcel of it.

If you believe we are headed for economic turmoil and that some of the problems I have described do exist in our society and economy, what are you going to do about it? While perhaps you can't take control of the government (although don't discount your vote and your voice), you can begin by taking control of your portfolio and financial future. Oliver Wendell Holmes may have said it best: "Prophesy as much as you like, but always hedge." So my friends, may you remain always invested, and always hedged.

# ACKNOWLEDGMENTS

This book would not have happened without my lovely, smart, and unerringly wise wife, Laura. Twenty years ago, she showed incredible faith in me and my crazy idea when she agreed to leave Houston and start Swan Global Investments in Durango, Colorado. Laura and my children repeated that faith and confidence in me when we all agreed to relocate to Puerto Rico.

Thanks to Alyssa, Kaitlin, and Christian Swan who demonstrated great support and patience as I spent hours and hours hunched over a computer writing *the book*. Despite a few eye rolls and "keep your voice down—Dad's on that book thing again," they could not have been more encouraging.

Much appreciation to Micah Wakefield, Portfolio Manager, Director of Research and Product Development at Swan Global Investments, who knew what was needed to keep this project going. Swan's Marc Odo, Client Portfolio Manager, and David Lovell, Managing Director of Marketing, played a huge part in putting this book together; it could not have happened without their work. Sean McCaffrey, Chris Hausman, Pat Stiefel, and my brother Rob Swan also made significant contributions.

I also want to thank the team at Greenleaf Book Group who helped ensure that no idea was left underdeveloped in my original manuscript nor any comma out of place.

A note of thanks also to the historical heroes of economic theory and individual liberty whose ideas created the American exceptionalism that we enjoy today. The framers of the Constitution gave us a free market, an individual-based blueprint for success. Economists and philosophers like John Locke, Friedrich Hayek, Alexis de Tocqueville, Ayn Rand, and Milton Friedman, to name a few, provided me and millions of others who understand the value of liberty with intellectual information that allows us to think about, explore, and utilize these important ideals.

Last, but not least, I am grateful to my parents for the values and lessons they taught me over the years. I would not be who I am or where I am without them.

# APPENDIX 1: OPTIONS 101

## What are options?

The textbook definition:

> An option is a financial derivative that represents a contract sold by one party (the option writer) to another party (the option holder). The contract offers the buyer the right, but not the obligation, to buy (call) or sell (put) a security or other financial asset at an agreed-upon price (the strike price) during a certain period of time or on a specific date (exercise date).[1]

Let's break down this definition into something bite-sized. There are only two types of options: calls and puts. Owning a call gives its holder the right to purchase an asset at a predetermined price (the strike price) even if the market price of the asset is much higher. Conversely, owning a put gives its holder the right to sell an asset a predetermined price, even if its market price is lower.

Generally speaking, the holders of a call option are bullish on the asset. They are hoping the asset goes up in value and that their call option allows them to acquire that asset at the lower price, i.e., the strike price. On the flip side, holders of a put option are generally bearish on an asset. If the market price of the asset falls, they will be able to sell it at the higher strike price.

Obviously, call options and put options are not free. On the other side of the transaction is the seller or "writer" of the option. The seller of the option takes on the obligation to provide the asset at the strike price if the asset's value goes up (in the case of a call) or agrees to purchase the asset at the strike price should the asset's value fall (in the case of a put).

Should the asset go past the strike price, the option writer will suffer a loss. To compensate the writer for this risk, the writer collects a premium. The probability of whether the option writer will suffer a loss determines the price at which they are willing to sell that option.

Option contracts also have an expiration date. When an option expires, it no longer has value and ceases to exist.

A common analogy for a put option is insurance. Most everyone carries insurance on their house, automobiles, health, and other significant sources of value. Should the value of an asset like an automobile go to zero following a nasty collision, the holder of the insurance policy will receive compensation; he or she has essentially "locked in" the sale price of the car if it becomes worthless. Obviously, there is a carrying cost to maintaining home, auto, and health insurance policies. The insurance company bears the financial risk of unfortunate events, so they demand a monthly, quarterly, or annual premium to compensate them for this risk.

Therefore, a put option can be described as being similar to insurance on a financial asset. If one holds a financial asset, one can protect its value past certain levels of losses by locking in a sale price. To maintain that protection, however, the holder of the asset must continuously purchase new put options once the existing ones expire. This is no different than an insurance policy holder having to send a check every quarter to maintain the policy.[2]

## How can options be used to manage risk?

In the following graph, we see a profit/loss diagram for the simplest form of investing: a buy-and-hold, long position in an asset. If one holds a traditional asset, the gains or losses correspond on a dollar-for-dollar basis with price moves in the asset. The relationship is linear: A $5 increase in the asset's price will make the investor $5 wealthier; a $5 drop in the asset's price will decrease the investor's wealth by $5. Nothing fancy about that.

## Figure A.1.1. Profit/Loss: Long an Asset @ $100

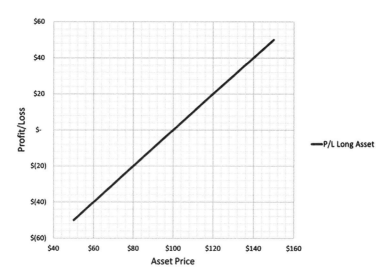

*Source: Swan Global Investments*

But what if the investor is bearish on an asset? What if the investor thinks the asset is overvalued and a price decline is imminent? Most developed markets allow an investor to short an asset. When shorting an asset, an investor sells an asset they technically do not own currently, under the promise of buying it back after an anticipated fall in value. The profit/loss diagram for a short position looks like this:

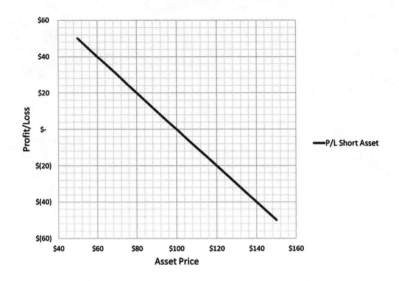

Figure A.1.2. Profit/Loss: Short an Asset @ $100

*Source: Swan Global Investments*

This graph doesn't take into account borrowing costs or margin costs, but the relationship is clear: The profit/loss diagram of a short position is exactly the opposite of a long position. A $5 decrease in the asset's price will make the investor $5 wealthier; a $5 increase in the asset's price will detract from the investor's wealth by $5.

And what if the investor wishes to avoid the vagaries of the market entirely? The common proxy for the "risk-free investment" is a short-term Treasury bill. As you can see in Figure A.1.3, the simplified profit/loss diagram for a short-term Treasury bill position, the profit is locked in at whatever the yield for that bill happens to be. Any movement in the market, up or down, has no impact on the profit or loss of the risk-free investment.

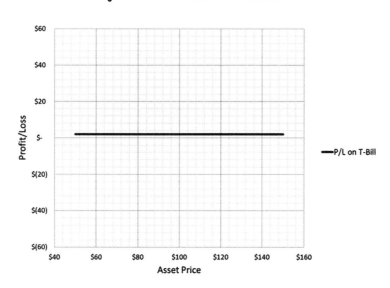

Figure A.1.3. Profit/Loss: T-Bill Yield at 2%

Source: Swan Global Investments.

The point of these three simple explanations is to illustrate just how limited traditional investors are when excluding the potential of options. A bullish investor can invest long, a bearish investor can invest short, and an investor wishing to avoid risk can invest in Treasuries. That represents a fairly limited toolkit.

Options allow us to expand our risk/return or profit/loss diagrams significantly. In Figure A.1.4, let us start with the simplest profit/loss diagram, that of the holder of a call option.

—————  Figure A.1.4. Profit/Loss: Long a Call @ $5 w/ $100 Strike Price  —————

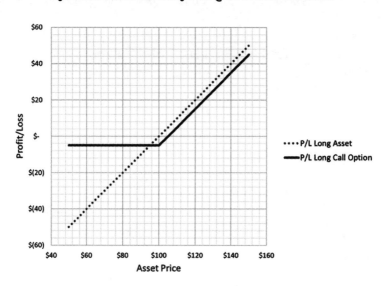

*Source: Swan Global Investments*

Here we see the option start off at a loss. Regardless of what the asset's final value will be, the premium paid represents a fixed cost to the buyer of a long call. That cost is paid at the outset, but the good news is the maximum loss of a long call position will never be more than the premium paid. Say, for example, an investor bought a call option for a premium or price of $5. Suppose the asset has a current value of $90 and the strike price on the option is $100. If that asset fell from $90 in value to $0 and the buyer of a long call paid $5 for the option, that $5 is all the downside they are really exposed to.

Conversely, the upside is theoretically unlimited. If the asset were to exceed its strike price, it goes in the money. The asset's market price could rise to $125, $150, $250, or more, and the investor holding a call option would be able to buy it at the bargain price of $100. Of course, the investor would still need to recover the original $5 cost incurred in order to turn a profit, but the gains are theoretically infinite in a long call position.

What about a long put option position? Remember, an investor holding a long put has a bearish disposition. They are expecting the value of the asset to go down. If the asset does fall significantly in value, the long put has essentially locked in a sales price for that asset. The further the asset falls in value, the more valuable the long put option becomes. In Figure A.1.5, we see the profit/loss diagram for a long put position.

### Figure A.1.5. Profit/Loss: Long a Put @ $5 w/ $100 Strike Price

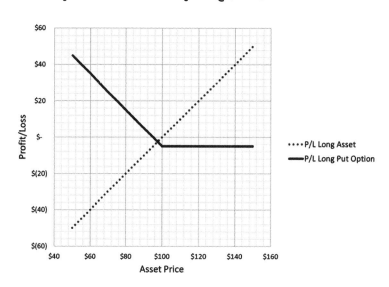

Source: Swan Global Investments.

The long put position is essentially the mirror image of the long call position, just flipped horizontally. As before, the premium paid to purchase the put is a fixed cost and represents the most the holder of a put option can lose in this particular trade. Let's assume in this case the asset has a current value of $110, the strike price is $100, and the premium is $5. If the investor is wrong and the asset goes up in value, the put will expire worthless and the investor loses the premium. It doesn't matter if the asset goes up to $101 or $500, the $5 premium is all the investor loses.

However, if the price of the asset falls to $75, $50, $25, or even nothing, the holder of the put option is able to force the counterparty in the trade to buy the asset for $100. The gap between the strike price and the actual price, less the price of the premium, represents the profit to the bearish investor owning a put option.

So those are the profit/loss diagrams of long calls and long puts, respectively. But what about the other side of the trade? After all, every buyer also has a seller. What do the profit/loss diagrams look like for someone to short a call or short a put?

Once again, the following diagrams look like mirror images, this time flipped vertically. If someone has sold a call or a put, the most they will ever gain will be the initial premium collected. The seller has to hold on and wait and hope that the option does not go in the money. A call option goes in the money if the asset's price is above the strike price and a put option goes in the money if the asset price falls below the strike price. Here are the profit/diagrams for both a short call and a short put position.

## Figure A.1.6. Profit/Loss: Short a Call @ $5 w/ $100 Strike Price

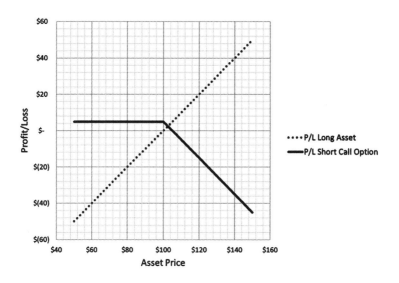

*Source: Swan Global Investments*

## Figure A.1.7. Profit/Loss: Short a Put @ $5 w/ $100 Strike Price

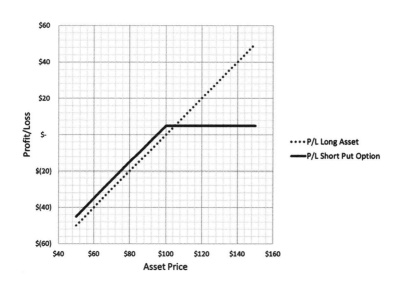

*Source: Swan Global Investments*

These four basic positions—long calls, long puts, short calls, and short puts—can be combined in countless numbers of ways. Positions can be mixed and matched to create all sorts of profit/loss diagrams. These positions can be taken for speculative reasons or risk-reduction reasons. Figure A.1.8 illustrates just a few of the various option strategies available.

## Figure A.1.8.

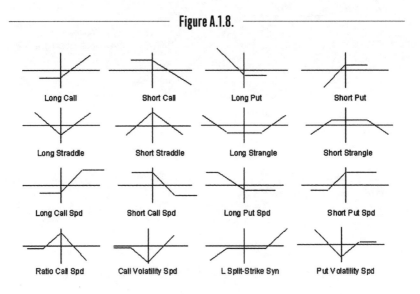

Source: *Swan Global Investments*

Obviously, there are a lot of options when using options. Entire books have been written describing the pros and cons of the various strategies illustrated above. The focus of this section is not to discuss the ins and outs of all of them. Instead, the point is to give you an idea of how the range of strategies and outcomes is much more diverse when incorporating the use of options.

# Why Would Anyone Sell Options?

If the profits of a short position are capped and the losses are potentially unlimited, why would anyone ever take a short position in an option trade? The answer is that it all comes down to probabilities. If it is highly unlikely that an option goes in the money, the seller of calls and puts can sit back and repeatedly collect premiums. Even if the occasional option does indeed go in the money, the seller does have some flexibility:

- The seller of options can make some adjusting trades to their original position to help minimize or recover losses.

- The seller of options hopefully has been successful enough on previous trades to have a "bank" of profits built up.

- If the probabilities shift to a higher likelihood of the short option trades going in the money, the seller can demand higher levels of premium for future trades.

Again, the analogy of insurance is a useful one. Returning to our previous example of home, auto, and health insurance, one might reasonably ask. "Why would any company agree to take on potentially huge losses by issuing insurance?" As it turns out, most insurance companies are experts at assessing risk and the probability of losses. They fully understand that there will be individual policies that they will have to pay out. But if they manage their risks right, there will be many, many more policies where they collect premiums for years and never have to pay a claim.

Moreover, in the aftermath of a crisis, insurance companies often increase the premiums they charge for a policy. After a hurricane blows through town, you typically see two things. First, more people rush to buy hurricane insurance as the disaster is fresh in their minds. Second, the premiums charged in this environment of heightened fear are usually higher. This allows the insurance companies to stay in business and literally weather the storm.

Most insurance companies have been around for decades, and some for centuries. They have remained in business due to playing the long game and having a big-picture, holistic view of risk.

In a similar vein, the writer of options must maintain a similar profile: Be cognizant of the worst-case risks, have an outstanding grasp of probabilities, and diversify risks across as wide a base as possible.

## How Has the Options Industry Grown and Evolved Over the Years?

Due to all the ways options can improve a portfolio's returns or mitigate its risks, the options industry has seen tremendous growth over the past few decades. In the early 1980s, 96.7 million contracts cleared, and daily volume exceeded around 500,000 contracts. By 2004 more than 1 billion contracts were traded and 4.1 billion in 2015. This equates to a daily volume of more than 16 million contracts.

The options market is also nicely spread across thirteen exchanges, and volume, pricing, and efficiency continue to improve.

## What Other Resources Can You Recommend that Discuss the Advantages and Uses of Options?

Here are some links to various research papers available for download from the Options Industry Council about the benefits of using options to manage risk and generate return:

**Risk Mitigating Collar Strategy**
https://www.optionseducation.org/content/dam/oic/documents/
institutional/research/cisdm-qqqactive-brochure.pdf

**Buy-Write Strategy for Fund Managers**
https://www.optionseducation.org/referencelibrary/research-articles/
page-assets/umass-buywrite-summary.aspx

**Risk Mitigating Collar Strategy: Option-Based Risk Management**
http://www.optionseducation.org/content/dam/oic/documents/
literature/files/options-based-risk-mgmt-summary.pdf

# APPENDIX 2: FURTHER READINGS

For those wanting more on the global debt problem, I have found these books to be helpful:

1. *The Game Is Rigged: How to Profit from the Coming Global Economic Collapse*, by Gregory Mannarino

2. *Endgame: The End of the Debt Supercycle and How It Changes Everything*, by John Mauldin and Jonathan Tepper

3. *The Death of Money: The Coming Collapse of the International Monetary System*, by James Rickards

4. *This Time Is Different: Eight Centuries of Financial Folly*, by Carmen M. Reinhart and Kenneth S. Rogoff

5. *Between Debt and the Devil: Money, Credit, and Fixing Global Finance*, by Adair Turner

6. *Government Is Killing the Economy! The Economic Impact of Regulation and Government Mismanagement on the U.S. Economy—Common Sense Thoughts on Finding A Cure*, by Walter Raquet

7. *The End of Alchemy: Money, Banking, and the Future of the Global Economy*, by Mervyn King

Swan Global Investments has a research team that publishes some great thought leadership. The following are links to our most popular white papers that are available on our website.

## The Swan Defined Risk Strategy (DRS): A Full Market Cycle Strategy

https://www.swanglobalinvestments.com/public/wp-content/
uploads/2018/07/white-paper-drs_-a-full-market-cycle-strategy.pdf

This paper discusses the Defined Risk Strategy (DRS) as a full market cycle strategy compared to a long-only strategy.

## Hope for the Best, Prepare for the Worst

https://www.swanglobalinvestments.com/public/
hope-for-the-best-prepare-for-the-worst/

This article breaks down some common misconceptions around bear markets, portfolio construction, and risk.

## The Retirement Conundrum: Untying the Gordian Knot

https://www.swanglobalinvestments.com/public/
retirement-conundrum-gordian-knot/

This paper dives into the daunting array of unique challenges investors in or soon entering retirement face, such as:

- The diminished role of public and private pensions and the greater importance of do-it-yourself defined contribution and IRA plans
- Increased longevity risk as people are living longer than ever before
- Bond yields at historic lows, threatening both the income and capital preservation roles of fixed income
- Stock markets at all-time highs while the global economy is slowing
- The risk of withdrawing from baby boomers' retirement accounts during bear markets in bonds and stocks
- The risk investors pose to themselves by panic-selling during market downturns

# Math Matters: Rethinking Investment Returns and How Math Impacts Results

https://www.swanglobalinvestments.com/public/math-matters/

Many investors make investment decisions based on emotions like fear and greed. They do not understand the math that drives successful long-term results and why this is important. Understanding the core mathematical principles driving investment returns can help investors make better investment decisions. These core principles are often overlooked, ignored, or misunderstood by investors and are explored in this executive summary paper for the purpose of strengthening the decision-making process.

# Diversifying with the DRS

https://www.swanglobalinvestments.com/public/
diversifying-with-the-defined-risk-strategy/

This paper reviews the DRS's goals, track record, and methodology, followed by a discussion regarding the logic of applying the DRS to additional assets and the practical implications of such an effort. The paper then shares back tests of the DRS applied to different assets and addresses potential challenges one might encounter when applying the DRS to asset classes other than US large-cap stocks. Finally, the paper discusses how diversification of multiple asset classes with the DRS applied could be used to build a better portfolio.

   To find more information and resources on the DRS and to receive updates of new papers, visit Swan's resource page at:

https://www.swanglobalinvestments.com/public/research-articles/

# IMPORTANT DISCLOSURES:

This communication is informational only and is not a solicitation or investment advice. Nothing in this presentation constitutes financial, legal, or tax advice. All information is subject to change or correction without notice. The charts and graphs contained herein should not serve as the sole determining factor for making investment decisions. To the extent that you have any questions regarding the applicability of any specific issue discussed to your individual situation, you are encouraged to consult with Swan Global Investments, LLC ("Swan"). All information, including that used to compile charts, is obtained from sources believed to be reliable, but Swan does not guarantee its reliability. Swan's investments may consist of securities which vary significantly from those in the benchmark indexes mentioned in this book and performance calculation methods may not be entirely comparable. Accordingly, comparing results shown to those of such indexes may be of limited use. All Swan performance results have been compiled solely by Swan Global Investments and are unaudited. Other performance return figures indicated in this material are derived from what Swan believes to be reliable sources, but Swan does not guarantee its reliability.

There is no guarantee the DRS structured portfolio investment will meet its objectives. This is not a guarantee or indication of future performance. References to the S&P 500 and other indices herein are for informational and general comparative purposes only. Indexes are unmanaged and have no fees or expenses. An investment cannot be made directly in an index. Investment strategies with other securities may vary significantly from those in the benchmark indexes listed. All investments involve the risk of potential investment losses as well as the potential for investment gains. Prior performance is no guarantee of future results and there can be no assurance that future performance will be comparable to past performance. Swan Global Investments, LLC, an independent Investment Advisory firm headquartered in Durango, Colorado, is registered with the U.S. Securities and Exchange Commission under the Investment Advisers Act of 1940. Being an SEC-registered advisor implies no special qualification or training. Swan offers and manages its Defined Risk Strategy to individuals, institutions, and other advisory firms. All Swan products utilize the Defined Risk Strategy ("DRS"), but may vary by asset class, regulatory offering type, etc. Accordingly, all Swan DRS product offerings will have different performance results due to offering differences and comparing results among the Swan products and composites may be of limited use.

There are eight DRS Composites offered: 1) The DRS Select Composite which includes non-qualified accounts; 2) The DRS IRA Composite which includes qualified accounts; 3) The DRS Composite which combines the DRS Select and DRS IRA Composites; 4) The DRS Institutional Composite which includes high net-worth, non-qualified accounts that utilize cash-settled, index-based options held at custodians that allow participation in Clearing Member Trade Agreement (CMTA) trades; 5) The Defined Risk Fund Composite which includes mutual fund accounts invested in the S&P 500; 6) The DRS Emerging Markets Composite which includes mutual fund accounts invested in emerging markets; 7) The DRS Foreign Developed Composite which includes all research and development account(s), and mutual fund accounts invested in foreign developed markets; 8) The DRS US Small Cap Composite which includes all research and development account(s), and mutual fund accounts invested in US small cap issues. Additional information regarding Swan's policies and procedures for calculating and reporting performance returns is available upon request. Swan claims compliance with the Global Investment Performance Standards (GIPS) and has prepared and presented this report in compliance with GIPS standard. Swan's compliance with GIPS has been independently verified from its inception on July 1, 1997 through December 31, 2018. A copy of the verification report is available upon request. To receive copies of the report please call 970.382.8901 or email operations@swanglobal-investments.com. Verification assesses whether (1) the firm has complied with all the composite construction requirements of the GIPS standards on a firm-wide basis and (2) the firm's policies and procedures are designed to calculate and performance is in compliance with the GIPS standards. Verification does not ensure the accuracy of any specific composite presentation.

The Defined Risk Strategy Select Composite demonstrates the performance of all non-qualified assets managed by Swan Global Investments, LLC since inception. It includes discretionary individual accounts whose account holders seek the upside potential of owning stock, and the desire to eliminate most of the risk associated with owning stock. The composite relies on LEAPS and other options to manage this risk. Individual accounts own S&P 500 exchange-traded funds, LEAPS associated with the ETFs, as well as option strategies based on other widely traded indices. The Defined Risk Strategy Select Composite includes all non-qualified discretionary accounts which are solely invested in the Defined Risk Strategy. The Defined Risk Strategy was designed to protect investors from substantial market declines, provide income in flat or choppy markets, and to benefit from market appreciation. Stock and options are the primary components of the strategy. The performance benchmark used for the Defined Risk Strategy is the S&P 500 Index comprised of 500 large-capitalization stocks, and which does not charge fees.

**Swan Defined Risk Strategy Select Composite**

| Year | Net-of-Fee Return | Composite Dispersion | Composite Assets (No. of Accounts / AUM in Millions) | Firm Assets in Millions | 3-Yr Annualized Standard Deviation | S&P 500 ("The Benchmark") Return | S&P 500 ("The Benchmark") 3-Yr Annualized Standard Deviation | 60% S&P 500/40% Barclays Aggregate Return | 60% S&P 500/40% Barclays Aggregate 3-Yr Annualized Standard Deviation |
|---|---|---|---|---|---|---|---|---|---|
| 1997 | 19.17% | - | <5 / .22 | 0.20 | - | 10.58% | - | 9.01% | - |
| 1998 | 11.55% | - | <5 / .32 | 0.31 | - | 28.58% | - | 20.98% | - |
| 1999 | 12.26% | - | <5 / .72 | 0.73 | - | 21.04% | - | 12.00% | - |
| 2000 | 3.17% | - | <5 / .90 | 0.93 | - | -9.10% | - | -0.99% | - |
| 2001 | 7.46% | - | <5 / 1.66 | 1.59 | 7.23% | -11.89% | 16.71% | -3.71% | 9.99% |
| 2002 | 12.22% | - | <5 / 1.97 | 1.92 | 10.20% | -22.10% | 18.55% | -9.82% | 10.77% |
| 2003 | -0.65% | 5.68% | 6 / 3.74 | 3.74 | 10.11% | 28.68% | 18.07% | 18.48% | 10.26% |
| 2004 | 12.28% | 5.80% | 7 / 4.45 | 4.66 | 9.94% | 10.88% | 14.86% | 8.30% | 8.49% |
| 2005 | 7.47% | 2.66% | 7 / 4.76 | 4.98 | 6.19% | 4.91% | 9.04% | 4.00% | 5.61% |
| 2006 | 18.14% | 3.71% | 9 / 7.22 | 7.76 | 4.60% | 15.79% | 6.82% | 11.12% | 4.33% |
| 2007 | 8.81% | 3.79% | 10 / 8.82 | 9.40 | 6.04% | 5.49% | 7.68% | 6.22% | 4.56% |
| 2008 | -4.50% | 5.00% | 12 / 12.15 | 15.65 | 9.54% | -37.00% | 15.08% | -22.06% | 9.48% |
| 2009 | 25.00% | 11.69% | 50 / 47.74 | 55.79 | 11.10% | 26.46% | 19.63% | 18.40% | 12.40% |
| 2010 | 8.10% | 2.13% | 71 / 86.09 | 97.90 | 10.93% | 15.06% | 21.85% | 12.13% | 13.56% |
| 2011 | -5.38% | 3.16% | 97 / 46.89 | 59.44 | 9.67% | 2.11% | 18.71% | 4.69% | 11.28% |
| 2012 | 9.01% | 1.73% | 276 / 97.52 | 400.19 | 7.65% | 16.00% | 15.09% | 11.31% | 8.64% |
| 2013 | 14.34% | 1.38% | 286 / 230.84 | 1,052.99 | 6.84% | 32.39% | 11.94% | 17.56% | 7.00% |
| 2014 | 6.52% | 0.47% | 372 / 315.14 | 1,810.04 | 4.83% | 13.69% | 8.97% | 10.62% | 5.48% |
| 2015 | -2.93% | 0.46% | 402 / 305.55 | 2,446.11 | 5.88% | 1.38% | 10.47% | 1.28% | 6.37% |
| 2016 | 9.59% | 0.58% | 566 / 379.28 | 3,620.08 | 5.46% | 11.96% | 10.59% | 8.31% | 6.33% |
| 2017 | 10.83% | 0.26% | 714 / 552.64 | 4,975.33 | 5.01% | 21.83% | 9.92% | 14.21% | 5.85% |
| 2018 | -7.74% | 0.36% | 582 / 430.65 | 4,063.88 | 6.44% | -4.38% | 10.80% | -2.35% | 6.38% |

# ENDNOTES

## Preface

1. "The Financial Crisis: This Day—One Year Ago, Sept. 29, 2008," CNBC, updated August 2, 2010, https://www.cnbc.com/id/33004978.

## Chapter 1

1. "Market Risk," Investopedia, https://www.investopedia.com/terms/m/marketrisk.asp.

## Chapter 2

1. "Natural Law," Investopedia, https://www.investopedia.com/terms/n/natural-law.asp.

2. Lawrence Goodman, "Demand for U.S. Debt Is Not Limitless," *Wall Street Journal*, March 27, 2012, https://www.wsj.com/articles/SB10001424052702304450004577279754275393064.

3. *Saturday Night Live*, "Don't Buy Stuff," https://www.nbc.com/saturday-night-live/video/dont-buy-stuff/n12020.

4. According to usdebtclock.org, referring to U.S. Treasury reported numbers, in 2017.

5.  Laurence Kotlikoff, "Oh, and By the Way, Our Government Is Totally Broke!" *Forbes*, October 7, 2013, https://www.forbes.com/sites/ kotlikoff/2013/10/07/oh-and-by-the-way-our-government-is-totally-broke/#772513e770c2.

6.  "Underfunded Pensions: Tackling an 'Invisible' Crisis," Knowledge@ Wharton (blog), January 26, 2015, http://knowledge.wharton.upenn. edu/article/underfunded-pensions-tackling-an-invisible-crisis/.

7.  Andrew G. Biggs, "The Hidden Danger in Public Pension Funds," *Wall Street Journal*, December 15, 2013, https://www.wsj.com/articles/the-hidden-danger-in-public-pension-fundsthe-hidden-danger-in-public-pension-funds-1387141006.

8.  Mark Niquette, Michael B. Marois, and Rodney Yap, "$822,000 Worker Shows California Leads U.S. Pay Giveaway," *Bloomberg*, December 10, 2012, http://www.bloomberg.com/news/articles/2012-12-11/-822-000-worker-shows-california-leads-u-s-pay-giveaway.

9.  "State cannot ignore pension problems," *The Day*, December 26, 2014, https://www.theday.com/article/20141226/OP01/312269982.

10. Steven Malanga, "Pension Sticker Shock," *City Journal*, March 26, 2015, https://www.city-journal.org/html/pension-sticker-shock-11541. html.

11. Romy Varghese, "Lifeguards Get Pensions? At Age 45? They Do in Atlantic City," *Bloomberg*, November 8, 2015, https://www .bloomberg.com/news/articles/2015-11-09/lifeguards-get-pensions-at-age-45-they-do-in-atlantic-city.

12. Mark Steyn, *After America: Get Ready for Armageddon* (Washington, D.C.: Regnery Publishing, 2011), 10.

13. Stephen Moore, "The Laffer Curve turns 40: the legacy of a controversial idea," *Washington Post*, December 26, 2014, https:// www.washingtonpost.com/opinions/the-laffer-curve-at-40-still-looks-good/2014/12/26/4cded164-853d-11e4-a702-fa31ff4ae98e_story. html?noredirect=on&utm_term=.0a21b43bc51a.

14. "Census Briefs—Households and Families: 2010," U.S. Census, issued April 2012, https://www.census.gov/prod/cen2010/briefs/c2010br-14.pdf.

15. Tax Policy Center, 2015.

16. U.S. Debt Clock, http://www.usdebtclock.org/index.html.

17. "Budget of the United State Government," Office of Management and Budget, https://www.gpo.gov/fdsys/browse/collectionGPO.action?collectionCode=BUDGET.

18. "Monthly Budget Review: Summary for Fiscal Year 2017," Congressional Budget Office, November 7, 2017, https://www.cbo.gov/publication/53286.

19. "Grover Norquist: The Interview," *The American Spectator*, https://spectator.org/51106_grover-norquist-interview/.

20. The Federalist Papers is a collection of essays written by Alexander Hamilton, James Madison, and John Jay to support and argue for the United States Constitution.

21. "Retirement Throughout the Ages: Expectations and Preparations of American Workers, 16th Annual Transamerica Retirement Survey of Workers," Transamerica Institute for Retirement Studies, May 2015.

22. John Carney, "The Size of the Bank Bailout: $29 Trillion," CNBC, December 14, 2011, http://www.cnbc.com/id/45674390.

23. "What is the purpose of the Federal Reserve System?" FAQs, U.S. Federal Reserve, https://www.federalreserve.gov/faqs/about_12594.htm.

24. Howard R. Gold, "Never mind the 1 percent: Let's Talk About the 0.01 Percent," *Chicago Booth Review*, Winter 2017, http://review.chicagobooth.edu/economics/2017/article/never-mind-1-percent-lets-talk-about-001-percent.

25. Jess Desjardins, "All of the World's Money and Markets in One Visualization," The Money Project, updated October 26, 2017.

# Chapter 3

1. It is important to note that this crisis preceded the dot.com bust by several years and just two years after the "irrational exuberance" speech by then-Federal Reserve chair Alan Greenspan.

2. Roger Lowenstein, *When Genius Failed: The Rise and Fall of Long-Term Capital Management* (New York: Random House, 2000), 42.

3. John Maynard Keynes, *The General Theory of Employment, Interest, and Money*, 1936.

4. Lowenstein, *When Genius Failed*, 52.

5. R.F. Harrod, *The Life of John Maynard Keynes* (New York: W.W. Norton & Company, 1951).

6. Lowenstein, *When Genius Failed*, 58.

7. Lowenstein, *When Genius Failed*, 68.

8. Lowenstein, *When Genius Failed*, 104.

9. Lowenstein, *When Genius Failed*, 61.

10. Lowenstein, *When Genius Failed*, 64.

11. Robert C. Merton and Myron Scholes are economists who, alongside Fischer Sheffey Black, originated the Black-Merton-Scholes options pricing models.

12. Lowenstein, *When Genius Failed*, 65.

13. "Moral Hazard," Investopedia, https://www.investopedia.com/terms/m/moralhazard.asp.

14. Subprime refers to a lower standard of borrower qualification and not interest rates.

15. Michael Lewis, *The Big Short: Inside the Doomsday Machine* (New York: W.W. Norton & Company, 2010), 9–10 and 13.

16. Lewis, *The Big Short*, 28.

17. "What did the 2008–10 Tax Stimulus Acts do?," Tax Policy Center, https://www.taxpolicycenter.org/briefing-book/what-did-2008-10-tax-stimulus-acts-do.

18. "Estimated Impact of the American Recovery and Reinvestment Act on Employment and Economic Output from October 2011 Through December 2011," Congressional Budget Office, February 2012, http://www.cbo.gov/sites/default/files/cbofiles/attachments/02-22-ARRA.pdf.

19. Meeting of the Federal Open Market Committee, U.S. Federal Reserve, October 23–24, 2012, https://www.federalreserve.gov/monetarypolicy/files/FOMC20121024meeting.pdf.

20. Minutes of the Federal Open Market Committee, U.S. Federal Reserve, October 23–24, 2012, https://www.federalreserve.gov/monetarypolicy/fomcminutes20121024.htm.

21. "Japan GDP Growth Rate," Trading Economics, https://tradingeconomics.com/japan/gdp-growth.

22. *Elliot Wave Theorist*, June 2018.

23. Yahoo Finance, S&P Total Return Index.

24. John Mauldin and Jonathan Tepper, *Endgame: The End of the Debt Supercycle and How It Changes Everything* (New Jersey: John Wiley & Sons Inc., 2011), ix.

# Chapter 4

1. "Pascal's Wager," Wikipedia, https://en.wikipedia.org/wiki/Pascal%27s_Wager.

2. Alan Hájek, "Pascal's Wager," *The Stanford Encyclopedia of Philosophy* (Summer 2018 edition), Edward N. Zalta (ed.), https://plato.stanford.edu/entries/pascal-wager/index.html.

3. Richard H. Popkin, ed., "Blaise Pascal," *The Columbia History of Western Philosophy* (Columbia University Press, 1999), 353.

4. "Stanley Druckenmiller: 'It's Going to End Very Badly" (Interest Rate Manipulation)," from interview on CNBC, DistressedVolatility. com, March 3, 2013, http://www.distressdvolatility.com/2013/03/ Stan-Druckenmiller-its-going-to-end-badly-so-much-price-manipulation.html.

5. "Stanley Druckenmiller: 'It's Going to End Very Badly" (Interest Rate Manipulation)."

6. "Waiting for Average: Why the Long-Term Average Will Never Occur for Today's Investors," Crestmont Research, updated April 2016, http://www.crestmontresearch.com/docs/Stock-Waiting-For-Avg.pdf.

7. Jessica Dickler, "Most Americans live paycheck to paycheck," CNBC, August 24, 2017, https://www.cnbc.com/2017/08/24/most-americans-live-paycheck-to-paycheck.html.

8. "Executive Order 6102," Wikipedia, https://en.wikipedia.org/wiki/Executive_Order_6102.

9. Bruce Stokes, "Global Publics More Upbeat About the Economy," Pew Research Center, June 5, 2017, http://www.pewglobal.org/2017/06/05/global-publics-more-upbeat-about-the-economy/.

10. Evan Osnos, "Doomsday Prep for the Super-Rich," *New Yorker*, January 30, 2017, https://www.newyorker.com/magazine/2017/01/30/doomsday-prep-for-the-super-rich.

11. "Warren, Sanders, Gillibrand, Markey, Harris, and Velázquez Unveil Debt-Relief Legislation for Puerto Rico, U.S. Territories," Senate. gov, July 25, 2018, https://www.warren.senate.gov/newsroom/press-releases/warren-sanders-gillibrand-markey-harris-and-velzquez-unveil-debt-relief-legislation-for-puerto-rico-us-territories.

12. Joel Kotkin, "America is moving toward an oligarchical socialism," Orange County Register, September 1, 2018.

13. "A Future That Works: Automation, Employment, and Productivity," McKinsey Global Institute study, McKinsey & Company, January 2017.

14. John Maynard Keynes, "Economic Possibilities for Our Grandchildren (1930)," from Keynes' *Essays in Persuasion* (New York: W.W. Norton & Company, 1963), www.econ.yale.edu/smith/econ116a/keynes1.pdf.

15. Source: McKinsey Global Institute study, 2017.

16. Joel Kotkin, "America is moving toward an oligarchical system," *Orange County Register*, September 1, 2018, https://www.ocregister.com/2018/09/01/america-is-moving-to-oligarchical-socialism/.

## Chapter 5

1. "Modern portfolio theory," Wikipedia, https://en.wikipedia.org/wiki/Modern_portfolio_theory.

2. Bernice Napach, "Bill Gross: Historic 40-Year Stock and Bond Run Is Over," *ThinkAdvisor*, June 3, 2016, https://www.thinkadvisor.com/2016/06/03/bill-gross-historic-40-year-stock-and-bond-run-is.

3. Christine Benz, "Experts Forecast Long-Term Stock and Bond Returns: 2018 Edition," Morningstar, interview with John Bogle, Vanguard Group, from October 2017. http://news.morningstar.com/articlenet/article.aspx?id=842900 Based on U.S. large cap equities and 50% U.S. 10-year Treasury and 50% U.S. corporate bond index.

4. "Capital market assumptions: Asset return expectations and uncertainty," BlackRock Inc., December 2018, https://www.blackrock.com/institutions/en-us/insights/portfolio-design/capital-market-assumptions.

5. Rob Arnott, Vitali Kalesnik, Jim Masturzo. "CAPE Fear: Why CAPE Naysayers Are Wrong," Research Affiliates, January 2018, https://www.researchaffiliates.com/en_us/publications/articles/645-cape-fear-why-cape-naysayers-are-wrong.html. Based on U.S. large-cap equities and Barclays U.S. Aggregate Bond Index. Arnott states their returns are forecast in real terms.

6. "2018 Long-Term Capital Market Assumptions," 22nd annual ed., J.P. Morgan Asset Management, September 2017, https://am.jpmorgan. com/gi/getdoc/1383498280832.

7. Benz, Christine "Experts Forecast Long-Term Stock and Bond Returns: 2018 Edition," interview with Morningstar Investment Management, September 2017.

8. State Street Global Advisors, "SSGA Long-Term Asset Class Forecasts," June 2018, https://www.ssga.com/content/dam/SSGA/ pdfs/macro-commentary/forecasts/2018/Long-Term-Asset-Class-Forecasts-20180630.pdf.

9. Michael Rausch, "10-Year Capital Market Return Assumptions," BNY Mellon Investment Management, 2017, http://www.bnymellonam. jp/wordpress/wp-content/uploads/2_BNY-Mellon-10yr-CapMkt-2017-WP.pdf.

10. Dalbar Inc., *Quantitative Analysis of Investor Behavior*, 2017.

# Chapter 6

1. Dalbar Inc., *Quantitative Analysis of Investor Behavior*, 2017.

2. "Press release: The Prize in Economic Sciences 2017," The Nobel Prize, October 9, 2017, https://www.nobelprize.org/prizes/ economics/2017/press-release/.

3. "Put Option," Investopedia, https://www.investopedia.com/terms/p/ putoption.asp.

# Chapter 7

1. Shlomo Benartzi, *Save More Tomorrow: Practical Behavioral Finance Solutions to Improve 401(k) Plans* (New York: Portfolio/Penguin, 2012).

2. Robert Thaler, *Misbehaving; The Makings of Behavioral Economics* (New York: W.W. Norton & Company, 2015).

3. Dalbar Inc., *Quantitative Analysis of Investor Behavior*, 2017.

4. Marc Odo, "Hope for the Best, Prepare for the Worst," Swan Global Investments, 2.

## Chapter 8

1. "Moneyness," Investopedia, https://www.investopedia.com/terms/m/moneyness.asp.

2. "Investment Outlook from Bill Gross," Janus Capital Group, June 2016, http://image.exct.net/lib/ff021270746501/m/9/40643+-+TL-Bill+Gross+Investment+Outlook_June+2016+JID_exp+06.30.17.pdf.

## Chapter 9

1. Randy Swan, *The Swan Defined Risk Strategy—A Full Market Cycle Strategy*, updated June 2016, 4, https://www.swanglobalinvestments.com/public/wp-content/uploads/2018/07/white-paper-drs_-a-full-market-cycle-strategy.pdf.

2. John Nyaradi, *Super Sectors: How to Outsmart the Market Using Sector Rotation and ETFs* (New Jersey, John Wiley & Sons Inc., 2010), 17.

## Appendix 1

1. "Option," Investopedia, https://www.investopedia.com/terms/o/option.asp.

2. For full disclosure, I am a member of the Options Industry Council's Advisory Council. The Advisory Council's mission is to support education about options within the financial advisor channel. The

Options Industry Council (OIC) exists as the primary educational arm of the options industry. I have enjoyed working with the various OIC team members over the past ten or so years, including Frank Tirado, OIC's vice president of education. I have also participated with other OIC representatives, Eric Cott and Alan Grigoletto, on numerous conferences and radio shows. Collectively, they have done a great job of bringing awareness to the investment community about the options industry regarding options' usefulness and educating investors about the opportunities available through options.

# INDEX

NOTE: Page numbers with *italic f* indicate a figure.

# ABOUT THE AUTHOR

Randy Swan is the founder, CEO and Lead Portfolio Manager of Swan Global Investments and the creator of the proprietary Defined Risk Strategy (Swan DRS).

In 1997, recognizing the limitations of Modern Portfolio Theory and the difficulty of market timing and picking stocks, Randy developed the Swan Defined Risk Strategy to help investors redefine the risk/return dynamic of long-term investing, seeking to achieve capital appreciation while seeking protection from large losses.

As Lead Portfolio Manager of Swan and the DRS, Randy oversees and manages the strategy across numerous product portfolios and asset classes such as large cap stocks, emerging market stocks, foreign developed stocks, small cap stocks, long-term bonds, gold, and more. Across each product/portfolio, the DRS strategy seeks to define the risk, reduce volatility, limit large losses and match or exceed the long-term performance of the stock market over an entire investment cycle (peak to trough). This is all from the perspective of helping investors to achieve a more consistent and smoother longer-term investment experience.

Before founding Swan, Randy was a senior manager for KPMG's Financial Services Group, primarily working with risk management and insurance providers. His experience at KPMG helped him in designing the DRS, as he was able to see firsthand how insurance and risk managers diminished risk. What followed was his discovery and pursuit of effectively using options as an investment vehicle to diminish and hedge risk. The DRS uses equities and options to define a particular risk/reward structure in portfolio management, thus seeking to mitigate large risks in portfolios and markets.

Randy has been featured in publications by *Barron's*, *The Wall Street Journal*, *Forbes*, *Morningstar*, *Investor's Business Daily*, and more. He has also been a frequent speaker at industry conferences including the Options Industry Council's Wealth Summit and the Alternative Investment Summit. Additionally, he serves on the Advisory Leadership Council of the Options Industry Council (OIC), an initiative designed to support education within the financial advisor channel, specifically focused on advancing the awareness and use of options in building a superior portfolio.

Randy is a 1990 graduate of the University of Texas with a master's degree in professional accounting.